The
TRUE
You

The
TRUE
You

A God's Eye View

Yakisha T. Simmons

Recommendations

This book will make you look inwardly and empower you to confront hidden and non-approachable views that are not always visible to the human conscious. Yakisha Simmons expounds on God's word through personal experience, practical application, and humor in a thought-provoking way, which keeps you wanting to read and discover more about yourself. If you are ready to see yourself as God sees you, and begin a new journey taking advantage of your privileges as a child of God, this is the book for you!!!

Pastor Christian Simmons, Exec. Pastor
New Bethel Sounds of Praise
Summerville, SC

Be prepared to receive insight and revelation that will lead you into a new dimension of spiritual truth in finding your identity through the plans and purposes that God has for your life. This wonderful book vividly captures the emotions of the writer of her receiving the revelation of the importance of knowing that no matter what you have done wrong or what did not go right in your life, know that you are who God says you are. I highly recommend this book.

Dr. Dee Dee Freeman, Sr. Pastor
Eyes of Faith Ministries - A Church on the Move Int'l
Waldorf, MD

Yakisha Simmons is committed to empowering women with not only a spoken word, but also a divinely inspired written word that teaches, motivates and challenges the reader to view themselves from the inside out rather than the outside in. Upon defining God's view of one's self, the reader is invited on a journey of self discovery inspired by biblical truths and supported by personal affirmations that ultimately equips one to live, demonstrate and express The True You in themselves. Well done!

Coach Anna McCoy, Author

Over the thirty-five years that I have been active in ministry, I've had the privilege of meeting thousands of people. It is almost invariably true that most of them are struggling with who they really are. This book, by Yakisha Simmons, is anointed to assist you in dealing with the "True You". I recommend that you read this book if you want to become more in touch with the person that God created you to be.

Dr. Edward Lee Johnson, Sr., Pastor, Author
Friendship Inspirational Church of God in Christ
Lincolnville, SC

Contents

Acknowledgements

Lord, I acknowledge you first and foremost, for it is You who leads me in the way that I should go. There is nothing that I can accomplish without the grace and favor of my Lord and Savior, Jesus Christ. Thank you, Lord, for using lil' ole me! I am humbled in your presence, and my heart longs to continue to please you and to encourage your people.

Thanks always to:

  ⁊ My dynamic and supportive husband, Jonathan, and to our two little men of God, Joel and Joshua, for allowing me the time to complete this project. You all bring me such joy! Every day the Lord gives me with you is more special than the last.

  ⁊ My parents, Donald and Sharon, who assisted me in this God-sized endeavor. I am just elated at the beauty of our relationships. I am amazed at how God can use the strangest things to confound the minds of even the wisest of men. I can never tell you enough how happy I am to have you as parents.

  ⁊ My wonderful father- and mother-in-law (and my pastors), Bishop Allen H. Simmons and First Lady Jan Simmons. I'm grateful for your constant prayers and support and for being the best in-laws a girl could hope for!

  ⁊ My grandmothers, Janie Johnson and the late Lizzie L. O'Bryant Pelzer (who departed this life for the glorious one in Heaven). You taught me so much about the Lord just in your everyday living. I will forever hold fast to your teachings and pray that one day my family will celebrate me as we do you.

  ⁊ My sisters, DeAndrea, Sadequa, Paola, Terry, Latitia and little Bethany. My heart swells with gratitude for all of you. People who do not need people...well, I certainly don't get that! Your smiles, encouraging words, hugs and even jokes add to the value of my life. I love you all and cherish your special places in my life. (Special thanks to Terry for lending her beautiful face for the front cover of this book.)

ဆ My brothers Carnell, Patrick, Allen, Christian, Jonathan, Michael, Marcel and little D.J. My father was the only male for a long time in our home, and for years, I secretly longed for brothers. Every day I thank God for your presence in my life. You are such men of God–wonderful examples for my two sons.

ဆ My nephew Aaron (A.J.). You are like a son to me, and I am so proud of you. You are a wonderful example of a well-balanced, God-fearing young man. Your presence in our lives was a blessing from the moment that you arrived, and I am excited about the GREAT things that God has in store for you. Keep making music for the kingdom and spreading the Good News of Jesus Christ!

ဆ All of my aunts, uncles, nieces, nephews, cousins, friends and my New Bethel Church family who all are such great supporters. It is so nice to know that there are some people in your corner who are cheering you on. God bless you all!

Special thanks to:

ဆ Dr. Alonzo Johnson and his beautiful wife, Richel, who impacted my life for many years. A pastor has a very unique calling, for you may be called to fill multiple roles in so many people's lives. Pastor Johnson, not only are you a spiritual leader, but you are also like a father to a lot of us (especially me!). The years that I spent under your spiritual tutorship has only enhanced my life. I love you and your family dearly. God bless you Pastor and First Lady!

ဆ My wonderful photographer, Dwight Davis. I hate to keep you all to myself, but we've got a good thing going! Why mess it up? God bless you, Da-white-around-your-lips!

ဆ Bernard 'BJ' Brown (Southern Wave Media). Thanks so much for sharing your gift with me. The cover is beautiful. Everything that you do, you do it well. You're going to soar, my brother.

Foreword

In reading the Scriptures, one is impressed with the frequent references describing Christians' identities in God. The Bible teaches us that every saved person is the object of a special, heavenly and effectual call. *The True You* takes us through the various themes of who we are in Christ.

As you read this book, your faith will increase, and you will begin to understand the benefits that are yours through Christ Jesus. Who you were designed to be will begin to become big in you as you read and meditate this text. No Christian has ever been called to "go it alone" in this walk of faith, and this book assures you of the myriad provisions–human and otherwise–that Christ has placed at your disposal as you grow in the knowledge of Him.

Minister Simmons inspires us to pursue who we really are in God, to trust His Word, and to believe that He will do what He said He would do. Thank you, Minister Simmons, for allowing God to use your talents for His glory!

Rev. Donald E. Bookard, Pastor
Welcome Travelers Missionary Baptist Church
Aiken, SC

Introduction

What is going *on*? That is the question I asked myself when the concept for this book was planted in the depths of my heart. There was this feeling of urgency that churned in my inner being. After hearing of the death of a friend by apparent suicide, I did a lot of assessing and noticed a few things that sincerely concerned me.

Over and over I would hear the voice of the Lord saying that there is a serious identity crisis taking place throughout the world. People really do not know who they are, and because of this lack of knowledge, the positive impact that the Lord could be having in their lives is limited. Misconceptions about our real identities are keeping us from a greater level of victory in our Christian lives. It is keeping us from tapping into the many blessings that the Lord has promised us as believers.

Many people are disillusioned and bamboozled by a cloudy view of themselves. This disillusion, which is manifested through our thought processes–based on internal and external experiences–creates and shapes our world. The maps of our destinies (skewed in our own minds because of disappointments, unfavorable outcomes and negative people) hinder and sometimes obliterate our journey to divine destiny.

It is the intent of the dark forces of this world to initiate feelings of inadequacy. When we embrace this emotion, we allow more of us to come under the influence of this powerful spirit. When it takes root, then we begin to live out the lie. This spirit convinces us that we actually belong under the cloud. We therefore become trapped–unable to wrestle free of this powerful spirit and eventually become void of purpose.

I must confess that I lived this way for a short time. I had a terrible self-image, but I can boldly testify today that I am indeed FREE! I was a people-pleaser. I wanted everybody to be happy, and I felt that it was my job to make it happen. This way of thinking affected me physically, emotionally, intellectually and spiritually. I would put everybody above myself and even above my family. I guess after growing up as a PK (preacher's kid) and then marrying a PK/Minister and serving others for so long, I had no clue where to draw the line.

It is the intent of the dark forces of this world to initiate feelings of inadequacy.

• • •

My identity rested in the happiness of other people. However, that was *not* my identity. God had a special plan for my life that only I could accomplish. I can only accomplish that which he has designed when I embrace my true identity the way that the Lord supernaturally created me to be.

The story of our newly elected president brings the premise of this book to the forefront. President Barack Obama could have allowed his background to dictate his identity. He came from a broken home. His father didn't have much of a presence in his life. His father was a black African and his mother a white American. These three things alone could have framed his way of thinking and could have shaped a distorted life for him. In addition, these seemingly negative details of his life could have been a catalyst for him to be a terrible husband, absent father, and have an aimless life. The blended color of his skin and having to choose one race to identify with could have caused him to seek comfort and solace in all the wrong places in an attempt to "fit in".

Notwithstanding, President Obama understood his true worth. He knew who he was and the value that was resident in him. His intrinsic value manifested as a loving husband and father and as a true leader and mentor to others. By understanding his gifts and abilities and against all odds, he became the first black President of the United States of America.

We weren't all called to be presidents, but do you know who you are created to be? Has your identity been erroneously shaped by circumstances and negative internal and external forces? As you read this book, find out who you really are, and embrace the true you. Begin to see through the eyes of God and see how beautiful He has made you. You are truly fearfully and wonderfully made! Once you have that knowledge embedded into your spirit, go forth and walk into your true destiny–free from the bondage of insecurity, insufficiency and negative self-worth.

Each chapter of this book reveals God's truth about you. The whole truth is that you are immaculately made in the image of our heavenly Father, whose only desire is for you to prosper through Him. *The True You* has a set plan that God wants to unfold in you. My prayer is that as you read these pages, you will begin to see yourself in a positive light and that you will bask in your God-given image by walking in it and by living it to the fullest!

After reading each chapter, speak aloud the confessions that confirm who you really are. Revisit and make these confessions often and especially when a lie is being whispered to you. Hide these words in your heart, and you will begin to notice a change in your perspective. Once you begin thinking differently, you can reshape your world into the world that you were designed to have–a life full of joy, peace and true prosperity!

• • •

Confession

Today, I discard forever the negative images that have shaped my identity for too long. From this day forward I walk and live in my true identity–understanding that God's purpose for my life is for me to walk in peace and victory. His purpose is for me to prosper physically, mentally, emotionally, spiritually and financially.

3 John 2

Beloved, I wish above all things that thou mayest prosper and be in health, even as thy soul prospereth.

• • •

Chapter 1
You Are the Righteousness of God

When you do not know who you are in God, you will not know your self-worth. You cannot live a life filled with joy and peace when you don't understand why you were created. It is impossible to have that deep and abiding joy of the Lord. You cannot reach your God-given potential in the spiritual nor in the natural. You cannot hear clearly from God when your mind is confused and when you're wrestling with self-doubt. Ultimately, these barriers will hinder you from ever accomplishing that which you were created to do.

When you do not know who you are, you will be easily distracted and misguided. Without much effort at all, you could be negatively influenced and manipulated. With no identity, you can easily lose your way, and you will ultimately just exist with no purpose, no goals and no vision.

As a testimony, that is how I lived for a while. I was sad and despondent for quite some time, because I was lost. I don't mean that I wasn't saved from my sins, but I couldn't grasp the next step in my salvation. I felt like an orphan, and my deficits kept me from embracing spiritually adoptive parents. This perpetuated the cycle and made me completely uncomfortable in my own skin. I knew that God's hand was on my life, but I could not access His plan because of my own identity crisis.

I was only an orphan in my own mind. On the contrary, I was so much more than that to my Father. Isaiah 61:10 states, "*I will greatly rejoice in the Lord; my soul shall be joyful in my God; for He hath clothed me with the garments of salvation, He hath covered me with the robe of righteousness, as a bridegroom decketh himself with ornaments, and as a bride adorneth herself with her jewels.*"

I am moved to tears when I think of all my delusions that my Savior covered with His robe of righteousness. Instead of making my imperfections known, he covered me in His love. He changed my garments with the garment that I was made to wear-- the garment that He designed for me and that completely changed my entire life!

This garment, the robe of righteousness, protects me from the enemy who comes to rob me of my joy and rightful position as a child of the Most High and a joint heir with Christ. This garment restores my pleasure in life and leads me down a path of fulfillment. The robe of righteousness establishes my dominion here on earth. This beautifully designed garment confirms my true identity as the beloved of my Father, and that I am truly precious in His sight.

• • •

The robe of righteousness establishes my dominion here on earth.

• • •

Because I now wear this robe, I can boldly say that I am the righteousness of God in Christ Jesus--and so are you! When we surrender our lives to the King, we take off those old garments, and He replaces them with the garments of salvation and the robe of righteousness. He does not stop there! He then adorns us with His precious ornaments of praise, adoration, joy, peace, and most importantly, His love.

Sometimes, even when we yield to the Spirit of God and allow Him to come into our hearts, we are often reminded of our past–either by an external or internal "old man" force. For quite a while, I could never get my mind off of any little mistake that I made. I am also keenly aware that often people hold grudges in their hearts when something is done against or to them that was not pleasant. Concern for others' contempt for me was a heavy burden that I carried from time to time, but I was my own worst enemy. I would beat up myself over and over about mistakes that I made. I would sincerely repent, but would continue to identify with the wrong that I committed. I would make this mindset my identity. I was no longer the righteousness of God but the girl who messed up.

I would wear that awful garment, not proudly, but like a coat that was made of heavy metal. It was a weighty, ugly garment. Reluctantly and dreadfully, I put that coat on daily. Yes, I knew the Scripture that stated, *"As far as the east is from the west, so far hath He removed our transgressions from us."* (Ps. 103:12). Needless to say, my mind was not renewed by the Word of God. Consequently, instead of embracing my new and true identity as a new creation in Christ Jesus and washed in the blood of the Lamb, I continued to identify with this negative perception of myself.

I can only imagine how annoyed the Lord would be with me when I constantly reminded Him of and repented for things for which He had already forgiven me. This reminds me of someone who would apologize every time we saw each other for something that happened years ago! As my discomfort grew each time I saw this person, the Lord allowed me to see myself. That is exactly how the Lord felt about me. Every time I would come before Him in prayer and repentance, I repented of the same things. It was not in worship nor in adoration but in pitiful repentance for things from my past that I had already been forgiven for!

I had to allow the Word of God to take root in my heart. Only then could I become truly free. Once my mind was renewed and I understood the hope of God's calling in my life (Ephesians 1:18), then I finally realized that when I have a heart that is truly repentant, and I turn toward God, I remove that undesirable garment, and He wraps me up in His garments of salvation and the robe of righteousness. Hallelujah!

God's attire is not weighty. The Bible says that His yoke is easy and His burden is light. (Matthew 11:30). So even if life throws you a few curve balls and the winds kick up some nasty dust (and they will), we have on our divine covering, and no guilt, self-doubt, nor condemnation can remove that robe! The Bible asks in Romans 8, *"Who can separate us from the love of God?"* Ask yourself this question. The answer is nothing. No thing. Not distress. Not persecution. Not family, friend nor foe. Nothing can separate us from His love. I call that real security!

Nor will He alter the thing that comes from His lips. When He adorned us with His robe, He had no intentions of taking it back. When He sees us wearing our divinely created garment, He smiles with love for His children. Our attire reflects our royal heritage in Him, and He receives the glory when He sees us walking out His will.

● ● ●

Our attire reflects our royal heritage in Him, and He receives the glory when He sees us walking out His will.

● ● ●

If others continue to remind us of the old garment that we used to wear, remember that you are the righteousness of God in Christ Jesus. You may have the same personality, because that is how you were uniquely made. However, your old pattern of doing things is null and void. You no longer think the way you did under the old man. Your actions and reactions are now dictated by the Holy Spirit which represents the New Man who is now in charge!

I periodically hear people say, "Hey, do you remember when you used to do this or when you used to do that (especially when they see you walking a new, redeemed path)?" There is nothing wrong with confidently affirming who you are now–the righteousness of God in Christ Jesus and adorned with His precious ornaments. You don't have to be deep. God knows I am not. The Bible says in 2 Corinthians 5:17, *"Therefore, if any man be in Christ, he is a new creature: old things are passed away; behold, all things are become new."*

All of us have fallen short. We are all born and shaped in iniquity. A child is never taught to lie, but when caught in a pickle, that very child will probably try to lie its way out of it. We've all struggled with sin. But if you confess Jesus Christ and have a heart of repentance, you are now walking a new, righteous path. Don't look back! The enemy often uses the past to thwart your future.

Are any of us really worthy of the righteous garments that God has freely given to us? The Bible answers this question in Isaiah 64:6: *"But we are all as an unclean thing, and all our righteousnesses are as filthy rags."* We who have been forgiven ourselves should always extend the same grace toward others, for it is the *gift of God*! Let's examine the following passage:

And one of the Pharisees desired Him that He would eat with him. And He went into the Pharisee's house, and sat down to meat.

And, behold, a woman in the city, which was a sinner, when she knew that Jesus sat at meat in the Pharisee's house, brought an alabaster box of ointment,

And stood at His feet behind Him weeping, and began to wash His feet with tears, and did wipe them with the hairs of her head, and kissed His feet, and anointed them with the ointment.

Now when the Pharisee which had bidden Him saw it, he spake within himself, saying,

This man if He were a prophet, would have known who and what manner of woman this is that toucheth Him: for she is a sinner.

And Jesus answering said unto Him, Simon, I have somewhat to say unto thee. And he saith, Master, say on.

There was a certain creditor which had two debtors: the one owed five hundred pence, and the other fifty.

And when they had nothing to pay, he frankly forgave them both. Tell me therefore, which of them will love him most?

Simon answered and said, I suppose that he, to whom he forgave most. And He said unto him, Thou hast rightly judged.

And He turned to the woman, and said unto Simon, Seest thou this woman? I entered into thine house, thou gavest me no water for my feet: but she hath washed my feet with tears, and wiped them with the hairs of her head.

Thou gavest me no kiss: but this woman since the time I came in hath not ceased to kiss my feet.

My head with oil thou didst not anoint: but this woman hath anointed my feet with ointment.

Wherefore I say unto thee, Her sins, which are many, are forgiven; for she loved much: but to whom little is forgiven, the same loveth little. And He said unto her, Thy sins are forgiven.

And they that sat at meat with Him began to say within themselves, Who is this that forgiveth sins also?

And He said to the woman, Thy faith hath saved thee; go in peace.

Luke 7: 36-50

There is a difference in gratitude of someone who has been forgiven of many sins versus someone who just committed a few sins and were forgiven as evidenced by this beautiful passage of Scripture. The woman with the alabaster box had heard of Jesus and, evidently, believed He was the Messiah. When she found He was so near to her, she took advantage of the opportunity to show her profound appreciation for His forgiving her many sins.

• • •

Our pasts are only important when we use them from which to learn valuable lessons.

• • •

The Pharisee was very judgmental and concluded that Jesus must not be a prophet, or He would have known she was a sinner. Notice in the text that Jesus *answered* Simon–although Simon did not actually speak. Jesus proved to Simon that not only was He a prophet by acknowledging that the woman was a sinner, but He also proved He was the Messiah by promptly forgiving her many sins! She was *much more* grateful because she was forgiven much.

This passage should serve as a constant reminder that our righteousness was freely given to us by Jesus Christ. Jesus died so that we could have the right to wear the precious garment of righteousness. This right was purchased for us by His precious blood. His blood wiped our slates clean and paved the way for us to regain access to our Father.

Our pasts are only important when we use them from which to learn valuable lessons. However, the *stain* of our pasts has been washed away by the blood of Jesus when we accepted Him as our Savior. If you have not yet accepted Jesus as Savior, I admonish you to do so *now*. You have an inheritance waiting for you to claim. It's all been bought and paid for, so all you need to do is accept it by faith. Only as a child of the Most High God can you qualify to wear the robe of righteousness. It's a gift. Just accept it!

We've examined the passage out of the New Testament that gives us a clear example of sins being exchanged for the robe of righteousness. Now let's examine the Old Testament. Zechariah was given a vision, and this is what he saw:

And He shewed me Joshua, the high priest standing before the angel of the Lord, and Satan standing at his right hand to resist him.

And the Lord said unto Satan, The Lord rebuke thee, O Satan; even the Lord that hath chosen Jerusalem rebuke thee: is not this a brand plucked out of the fire?

Now Joshua was clothed with filthy garments, and stood before the angel.

And he answered and spake unto those that stood before him, saying, Take away the filthy garments from him. And unto him he said, Behold, I have caused thine iniquity to pass from thee, and I will clothe thee with change of raiment.

Zechariah 3: 1-4

> • • •
> **Walking in the Spirit simply means agreeing with what God says.**
> • • •

Did you get this? The Lord has caused your iniquity to pass from you! Hallelujah! Once those old garments are removed, no matter the accusation, do not put them back on! One of the names of Satan is "the accuser of the brethren". He will bring accusations against you until Jesus returns. Allow the Word of God to take root in your heart that you are His righteousness. *"There is therefore now no condemnation to them which are in Christ Jesus, who walk not after the flesh, but after the Spirit."* (Romans 8:1)

Stay in the Spirit, and you will not be fooled by the condemnation of Satan. Walking in the Spirit simply means agreeing with what God says. If He says you are the righteousness of God, then bless God, believe it! Make a decision to live in victory!

The robe of righteousness was tailor-made for you. Every thread and button on your robe was handpicked for you. It was made to your unique specifications. It is not too long or too short. You don't have to be measured for it. Just pick it up, and put it on. You take off the old garment when you confess Him as your Savior, and in exchange, He gives you His righteousness. It's as simple as that.

Daily remind yourself that you are God's righteousness. Look at it over and over again in the Word. The more you look at it and confess it, the more you will walk in it. And since the Word is a mirror, you will soon reflect the image of God. You were already made in His image. Just as film from a camera has an image on it when a picture is taken, it has to be developed to see the picture clearly. Allow the Word of God to develop you and show you who you really are!

• • •
Confession

I am the righteousness of God in Him (Jesus). I am clothed in His righteousness. I no longer wear the ugly and weighty garments of sin and of my past. I am a new creation in Christ Jesus. I have been set free from bondage, and I now live a new and victorious life.

Job 36:7

He withdraweth not His eyes from the righteous; but with kings are they on the throne; yea, He doth establish them forever, and they are exalted.

• • •

Chapter 2
You Are Beautiful

David proclaimed in Psalm 139:14, *"I will praise thee; for I am fearfully and wonderfully made: marvellous are thy works; and that my soul knoweth right well."* Based on this proclamation, we can conclude that David recognized and understood that he, a human being intricately created and exquisitely assembled, was a spectacular creation that the Lord made!

"Wonderfully" in some versions of the Bible is translated "beautifully." I like that. We are *beautifully* made. The Lord imagined us, spoke faith-filled words, and we were crafted, every one of us, into His image (from His imagination). An image is the replica of the real thing, so He made us just like Him. Everything that the Lord made is *good*!

What is beauty?

The Random House Unabridged Dictionary defines beauty as "a characteristic present in a person, place, object or idea that provides a perceptual experience of pleasure, meaning or

> • • •
> The Lord imagined us, spoke faith-filled words, and we were crafted, every one of us, into His image.
> • • •

satisfaction to the mind or to the eyes, arising from sensory manifestations such as a shape, color, personality, sound, design or rhythm."

Too often what is beautiful to most people is often characterized by the sensory manifestation evoked by sight. The adage that "beauty is only skin deep" stems from the perception that what you see on the outside is not necessarily the same on the inside. Nonetheless, when Jesus came into our lives, His transforming power can make us beautiful inside and out!

When I was 16 or 17 years old, I represented the South Carolina Jurisdiction of the Church of God in Christ (COGIC) at a youth pageant. My dad, mom and younger sister, Sadequa, and I drove from South Carolina to Milwaukee, Wisconsin for the week-long event. It was an incredibly long car ride from which my sister and I thought we would never recover; but, I was eager to get there to meet other young people who were representing their respective jurisdictions.

Shortly after arriving at our destination, I searched for my Sunday School sponsor who immediately rushed me into a conference room that was already occupied by the other contestants. After a day of awkward conversations, the group of contestants from all across the U.S. began to enjoy one another's company. By the end of the second day, we were all inseparable–eating most of our meals together and sharing stories about our own little worlds. One of the contestants revealed that her first impression of one of the other contestants was horribly inaccurate. Her initial thought upon meeting the young lady was that she was shy and reserved, but to the contrary, she became the life of the entire group!

That admission sparked even more confessions about what we all thought about one another. The group eventually disclosed that they erroneously thought upon seeing me for the first time with my beautiful "mother" (who was not my mother, but my Sunday School sponsor, who is indeed beautiful inside and out) that I was stuck up and that they would not like me.

After a few minutes of shocking silence (literally, you could hear a pin drop), we all fell over laughing hysterically at the absurdity of it all. At that moment we all acknowledged how just looking at someone may not accurately define a person, nor can you determine their inner beauty by just a glance. We were all blessed to get to know the beauty of one another's individual personalities and the uniqueness in which we were all crafted.

You are beautiful, not because of how you look on the outside, but because of who made you and His proclamation over you. The creation is always defined by the creator. If our Creator declares in His Word that we are beautiful, then we should always declare ourselves beautiful–because He says so.

> • • •
> You are beautiful, not because of how you look on the outside, but because of who made you and His proclamation over you.
> • • •

The reason we often feel condemned, unloved, depressed, etc., is because we acknowledge what others call us rather than what our Creator called us. Genesis 1:27 states, *"God created man in His own image, in the image of God created He him; male and female created He them."* What an awesome and exceptional God we serve! We often sell ourselves short–not recognizing the significance of our very existence. Look in the mirror of the Word, and see yourself in His image–the very image of the eternal and only wise God, the Creator of heaven and earth; our heavenly Father-- God Himself!

I didn't make this up. Read it for yourself. This is not an unbelievable concept. When I run into my relatives, most of them say that I am the splitting image of my dad. I am not surprised at their declaration, because the seed of my dad was used to create me. I am made in his image because he is, well, my father!

My father here is my earthly dad. God is my heavenly Father–who actually also made my earthly father! So it stands to reason that we all are made in His image. The Bible declares in 1 John 3:2, *"Beloved, now are we the sons of God, and it doth not yet appear what we shall be: but we know that, when He shall appear, we shall be like Him; for we shall see him as He is."* When Jesus returns, we will see our Father just as He is and *we shall be like Him.*

What does this mean? It means that since the fall of man in the Garden of Eden, we were all stripped of our heavenly bodies and we were "born in sin and shaped in iniquity". When Jesus came, He redeemed us from the curse of the law. When we accepted Him as our Savior, He returned us to right standing with our Father, and our Spirits were immediately made righteous as in the Garden of Eden.

However, our souls (mind, will and emotions) and our bodies are being renewed daily through the washing of water by the Word. (Ephesians 5:26). We have to continually sanctify these two entities by reading and meditating on the Word of God and walking out what we believe. That's why Paul said in 1 Corinthians 13:12, *"For now we see through a glass, darkly; but then face to face: now I know in part; but then shall I know even as also I am known."*

We cannot see with our natural eyes exactly how we look like our Father. That's why we have to rely on His Word to us to claim that promise. But when Jesus comes back, our eyes will be opened, and we shall see Him *like He is,* and we will see that we look exactly like Him.

It is so important that we know we were made in His image. Society has drilled it into us that if you're not pretty enough (by their standards I might add), or if you're not tall enough, skinny enough, etc., that you're not socially acceptable. I beg to differ. If you are made in His image, you look exactly like you're supposed to look. If you want to change some of the features you were born with, it should be because it is something *you* desire and not because you feel pressured by society to do so. If you were born beautiful by the world's standards, then thank God, and don't allow anyone to make you feel guilty about it. We were all born with purpose and set into our families for His glory.

It is important to note that all of us will either have to die or be caught up to meet Him. It won't matter whether you're ugly, beautiful, poor, rich, young or old. Natural beauty, money nor fame will matter when we go before our Maker. If He has made us beautiful, then revel in your God-given beauty!

This outside shell will one day fade away, so don't put much stock in it. Strive to be transformed from the inside out by the Word of God. The heart of a man should be what is evaluated, and we are not even capable of doing that. The Bible says that *we* look on the outward appearance, but God looks at the heart. Allow yourself to be led by the Spirit of God, and His Spirit will see with clarity what is in another's heart. Always look at yourself and others through the eyes of the Spirit. If you don't, that old garment will try to come back on you and all of the characteristics with it: judgmental spirit, depression, envying, strife, etc. Don't go *back*. Go *forward*.

● ● ●

Get to know the *true you*– the person God created you to be.

● ● ●

Get to know the *true you*–the person God created you to be. The next time you doubt your beauty, remember you were made in His image. He made all things beautiful. The enemy has perverted some of it because of our sin nature, but the One who made you can put you back on the potter's wheel and refashion you into who you are called to be! Think about it. He chose *you* to look like *Him*. *"And God saw everything that He had made, and behold, it was very good."* (Genesis 1:3). You are a marvelous work of art!

I have taken a proactive approach with my children in showing them who they are. I know that the enemy, Satan, our adversary, will try to make them feel inferior, and at some point, they may doubt the reason of their very existence. I know this can happen, because I experienced it myself. So, I do what God commanded the children of Israel to do in Deuteronomy 6:6, 7: *"Write these commandments that I've given you today on your hearts. Get them inside of you and then get them inside your children. Talk about them wherever you are, sitting at home or walking in the street; talk about them from the time you get up in the morning to when you fall into bed at night."* (The Message)

As a confession, I have my two sons, 5-year old Joel and 3-year old Joshua, recite, "I am fearfully and wonderfully made." I must admit, it is extremely funny to hear them recite this confession because "fearfully" and "wonderfully" are not exactly words that such young children can pronounce. Even though they are too young to understand precisely what they're saying and the significance of these words, I know that their confession of God's Word causes their spirit man to be built up.

When this Word is rooted deeply within them, they will not be confused about their identity. When Satan tries to attack their minds – and he certainly will – the Holy Spirit will remind them of the Word that they already have on board. They can then cast down the false images that Satan tries to plant in their minds. They can speak the Word that opposes Satan's lies and bring into captivity every thought to the obedience of Christ. (2 Corinthians 10:5)

You may say that I'm rearing my children to be arrogant. Remember, walking in the Spirit is simply agreeing with what God says. If God says we are fearfully and wonderfully made, then I won't be arrogant if I agree with Him. I really believe it is pure arrogance *not* to agree with Him. After all, He is God, and He made everyone and everything. Who are we to disagree with *Him*? I believe *God*.

When we know who God made us to be, we can make better decisions, move forward boldly and have a victorious life. We can squash doubt and low self-esteem with the words that we speak out of our mouths. We can trample on negative mind sets, negative stereotypes, and yokes that others try to put on us. Just proclaim who God says we are and our steps will be ordered by the Lord.

This chapter was very important to me. I work with the youth at my church and in my community, and I have encountered

● ● ●
When we know who God made us to be, we can make better decisions, move forward boldly and have a victorious life.
● ● ●

young people with such great potential who have literally padlocked themselves into a negative mind set because of their own destructive thinking and because of negative comments by people who should be encouraging them to grow closer to God. Words are powerful containers. Only use words that edify, exhort, and comfort. Only *receive* words that edify, exhort and comfort you. Christ died so that you may have abundant *life*!

Don't compare yourself to others. When you do, you in essence are saying to God, "Lord, you made a mistake!" Only compare yourself to truth, and God's Word is truth. Everything else is a lie that was orchestrated to keep you in bondage. God made you someone special. God made you truly *beautiful*. Take what He has given you, and adorn it for His glory. Dress like you're a child of the King, for indeed you are!

Real change occurs from the inside out and not the outside in. Accept Christ as your Lord and Savior by asking Him to come into your life. Acknowledge that you believe in Him, and then grow in His knowledge through meditation of His Word and through fellowship with other believers. You will truly be transformed from the inside out, and others will begin to notice a light that surrounds you. Your transformation will leave an indelible impression on those around you.

It is my desire to see you walk in victory. Change how you think towards yourself. In order to change your thinking, you must change the way you speak. Only say what God says (agree with Him). Begin to say what my sons proclaim so proudly–*I am fearfully and wonderfully made*!

● ● ●

Confession

I am fearfully and wonderfully made. I am a work of art–crafted and drafted by the master craftsman. I was made in the image of the AWESOME Creator, and everything that God made is good! The Lord is pleased with me. He looks upon me with love and affection. I can boldly live my life knowing that God's loving gaze is always upon me.

Psalm 145:9

The Lord is good to all: and His tender mercies are over all His works.

● ● ●

Chapter 3
You Are A Friend

I often think about the sacrifice that Jesus made for us–giving His life to redeem us from the curse of the law with no assurance that we would even accept His gift. And then there was the fact that we could do absolutely nothing to repay Him. It reminds me just how much we owe Him.

In today's society, we all identify (some more than others) with being in debt. One thing that is clear is that most debts are not forgiven without a penalty–either your credit rating takes a beating or your reputation is damaged to the point that you can no longer borrow money. You may find that you cannot buy a home or finance a car at a low interest rate. A negative credit score or questionable credit history could even hinder someone with otherwise exceptional qualifications from obtaining certain employment opportunities.

Family members often stop speaking to one another when a debt is owed, and close acquaintances become distant when money is involved. Therefore, it truly humbles me to hear that God, my Savior and Redeemer, refer to me as His friend with such an overwhelming debt between us. The Bible uses many terms to compare us to the relationship that we have with Father God–child, heir, son, sheep and disciple, to name a few.

● ● ●

There is just something so special about being called a friend of God.

● ● ●

However, there is just something so special about being called a friend of God.

We don't get a choice of whether it's a girl or a boy when we have a baby. Nor can we choose our relatives. Even if a relative appears to be the worst individual morally, we can never disown them as blood, because it shows up in our DNA. (I watch CSI quite a bit, so I know what I'm talking about here.)

Thank God we can choose our friends. You may select friends based on their personalities or things that you share in common. You may enjoy the same pastimes, or you may just feel comfortable sharing your innermost thoughts, dreams and inhibitions. Your chosen friend provides a refuge of security and trust that allows you to let your hair down and open yourself to receive suggestions and criticism in a way that you couldn't receive from anyone else.

I was reminiscing the other day about the beautiful friendships that the Lord has blessed me with over the years. I am sometimes amazed that some of my childhood girlfriends and me have a special bond that has not been shaken by the passing of time or by the changing of life structures. I am still moved to tears when I think of my wonderful friends that traveled for miles to be with me on my wedding day. I have even found that neither distance nor time apart seems to affect the sincere fondness we share with and for each other.

I have cried to some of these very friends about a problem or shared some very intimate details of calamities that I have experienced, and they have done the same with me. I have crawled out of my bed late at night to console them and minister to them, and I have also driven distances to hold their hands when tragedy struck. When I need someone to listen to, they are there. When I need a good scolding, they do it in love and sincerity for my good. When I am blessed, they are just as happy as if it happened to them.

Of course, misunderstandings have occurred and will continue to occur. That is the nature of any kind of relationship. I have found, though, that true friends are more accepting and forgiving. When a friendship has not been forged, a relationship can easily be severed by conflict. I have even seen what seemed like solid marriages fail over a problem of which friends can easily forgive. *"A friend loveth at all times."* (Proverbs 17:17)

A friendship is a beautiful relationship. It is one of the closest associations that two people can share. Friends share deep secrets and a trust that every person should experience at least once in a lifetime. Only then can you truly understand how deeply Jesus regards such a relationship with us. I am honored that the Lord Himself calls me His friend! I am elated that I have a confidante such as Jesus, the Christ, the Son of the Living God! The New Living Translation (NLT) of Prov. 18:24 reads, *"There are 'friends' who destroy each other, but a real friend sticks closer than a brother."*

• • •

Jesus is a true friend in every sense of the word. When all other relationships fail or waiver, Jesus is always there with you and with me.

• • •

Jesus is a true friend in every sense of the word. When all other relationships fail or waiver, Jesus is always there with you and with me. I am sure it saddens Him when He doesn't hear from us, but He's always delighted when we return to Him and begin to commune with Him. We can talk to the Lord daily with no disquiet that our business will be the next hot topic on the gossip circuit. He loves to be in our presence, and I can honestly say that I love to be in His presence. His friendship is the most important relationship that I cultivate in my life.

Part of knowing who you are is to know that God truly

loves you and finds pleasure in being with you. He values your friendship–just as a true friend does. Here are some attributes of a friend that you will always find in Jesus:

- *He loves to see you do well.* "Beloved, I wish above all things that thou prosper and be in health, even as thy soul prospereth." (3 John 2)

- *He will never belittle you to your enemies.* "Thou preparest a table before me in the presence of mine enemies." (Psalm 23:5)

- *His presence will bring you comfort during a crisis.* "Fear thou not; for I am with thee: be not dismayed; for I am thy God: I will strengthen thee; yea, I will help thee; yea, I will uphold thee with the right hand of my righteousness." (Isaiah 41:10)

• • •

Part of knowing who you are is to know that God truly loves you and finds pleasure in being with you.

• • •

- *He will fight for you.* "But thus saith the Lord, Even the captives of the mighty shall be taken away, and the prey of the terrible shall be delivered: for I will contend with him that contendeth with thee, and I will save thy children." (Isaiah 49:25)

- *He will always have compassion towards you--even if you mess up.* "But He, being full of compassion, forgave their iniquity, and destroyed them not: yea, many a time turned He his anger away, and did not stir up all his wrath." (Psalm 78:38)

- *He will be there for you when you call Him.* "For whosoever shall call upon the name of the Lord shall be saved." (Romans 10:13)

- *He will not disappoint you.* "Be strong and of a good courage, fear not, nor be afraid of them: for the Lord thy God, He it is that doth go with thee; He will not fail thee, nor forsake thee." (Deuteronomy 31:6)

- *He does not hold grudges.* "Who is a God like unto thee, that pardoneth iniquity, and passeth by the transgression of the remnant of His heritage? He retaineth not His anger forever, because He delighteth in mercy." (Micah 7:18)

You are special to the Lord. The true you is a friend of God. You are not just a servant–created only to jump at His every command and to do His bidding like a common slave. A slave does not know the heart of his master. A servant is never privy to the personal or business matters of his owners: *"Henceforth I call you not servants; for the servant knoweth not what his lord doeth: but I have called you friends; for all things that I have heard of my Father I have made known unto you."* (John 15:15)

● ● ●

The true you is a friend of God.

● ● ●

Jesus values His relationship with you so much that every family or business revelation that is given Him by His Father is passed on to you. As blood-bought, heirs of salvation, He reveals His mysteries to us that He would never reveal to anyone else. Jesus was conversing with His disciples after having taught parables to the multitudes. The disciples wanted to know what the parable was all about. Jesus said to them, *"Unto you it is given to know the mystery of the kingdom of God: but unto them that are without, all these things are done in parables."* (Mark 4:11)

A true friend would never divulge secrets nor would family business be available to everyone. Jesus tells us secrets that others would not be able to understand–just like a friend does! He loves you so much that He wants to share everything with you. He has opened His world up to you. In His Word, He has revealed the intimate details of His heart with you: *"Call to me and I will answer you and tell you great and unsearchable things you do not know."* (Jeremiah 33:3). What a friend we have in Jesus!

Just as we rely on our Father's unconditional love, we must also extend grace to one another. Every relationship takes work, commitment, trust and loyalty. Just as we spend significant time with our friends here on earth, we should spend even more time with our Friend who is in Heaven. *"A man that hath friends must show himself friendly,"* according to Proverbs 18:24.

Being friendly is a simple act of lowering your will to accommodate someone else so that they can share their world with you in a comfortable atmosphere while they do the same for you. Friendship was ordained by God, so it must be pretty important. God shows us how to be a true friend in His Word, and He wants us to sow seeds of friendship wherever we go. The harvest will bring Him glory.

Forgiveness is key in a relationship. Jesus modeled it throughout His life here on earth. God sent His son so that we could be forgiven! He forgave us our trespasses, and He expects us to forgive others their trespasses. Every friendship will be tried. You will know the depth of the friendship when it is tested. Jesus was tested when it came time to prove His love for us. The depth of His love for us was shown when He died on the cross. Now that's a FRIEND!

We probably won't be tested by having the chance to give our natural lives for our friends, but we will certainly have to give up something. Friendship requires patience, love, endurance, and it sometimes requires sweat and wounds! *"Faithful are the wounds of a friend."* (Prov. 27:6). All of these characteristics were modeled by Jesus for us.

The role that Job's friends played in his life changed when Job began to experience difficulties. Instead of encouraging him and being a blessing physically and financially for Job, they began to analyze why Job was going through his trials and came to the conclusion that it must have been something he did that served as a catalyst for his affliction. Don't you just love friends like his?

After God spoke with Job a while, Job realized that he thought he knew God, but he found out that he really didn't! Once he embraced the proper perspective of God, the Lord turned his situation around when he prayed for his friends. That's what true friends do. They're not easily offended. Their aim is to restore the relationship, so they do whatever it takes to do so. Although Job's friends let him down, he continued to lift them up!

> • • •
> God loved us so much that He sent the ultimate friend to establish us as a people to Himself.
> • • •

Isn't that how God is? We often let him down, but he reaches down and lifts us right back up. God loved us so much that He sent the ultimate Friend to establish us as a people to Himself. This unselfish act provided us an entrance into heaven and an opportunity to have a relationship with Him on earth. He threw all of our sins into the sea of forgetfulness, so that we can come confidently to Him to share everything that we're going through with Him and so that He can share His plans for us.

You are a friend of the Most High God!

• • •
Confession

I am a friend of God. He loves me and values his connection with me. He is my confidante. He reveals His heart to me. Our special friendship confirms my identity and gives me hope for the future. I look forward to each day that we share together in this life and the life to come.

1 Samuel 19:3

And I will go out and stand beside my father in the field where thou art, and I will commune with my father of thee; and what I see, that I will tell thee.

• • •

Chapter 4
You Are Anointed

Knowing who you truly are means knowing that you are an anointed vessel of God.

The Bible says in 1 John 2:27, *"But the anointing which ye have received of Him abideth in you..."* When we accepted Jesus as our Lord and Savior, we allowed Him access into our hearts. Since Jesus is the Anointed One and the Anointed One abides within us, then we are anointed.

I have noticed that the "anointing" is often misrepresented, because it is frequently used to define someone who is extremely gifted or talented. I hear the term more often when referring to a person who has extraordinary musical or speaking abilities in a church setting. Generally, if a musician, singer, dancer or speaker can move a crowd of people to dance or to worship, they are often labeled "anointed". Everyone else, it appears, just exists and is not privy to the anointing of the Holy Spirit.

I was a believer of this misconception for quite some time until 1 John 2:27 was brought to my attention by the Holy Spirit. Because of this passage of Scripture, I now understand that each and every member of the body of Christ is endowed with Christ's anointing. I am anointed. If you name the name of Christ, *you* are anointed. As previously said, when you accepted Jesus Christ (Jesus, the Anointed One) as your personal Savior, you accepted Him into your heart. You invited the Holy One of Israel, the Anointed One to dwell in you. Just as the Scripture states, the anointing abideth in you.

Though my last name has changed since marriage, the blood that runs through my veins confirms my biological heritage. I will always be connected to the family in which I was born. My DNA has similar characteristics of the DNA in my dad, mom and siblings. In this same way, the blood of the Anointed One supernaturally transforms me into an anointed vessel. It confirms who I am in Christ Jesus. It was predestined for me to be endowed with this precious anointing.

> *"Blessed be the God and Father of our Lord Jesus Christ, who hath blessed us with all spiritual blessings in heavenly places in Christ. According as He hath chosen us in Him before the foundation of the world, that we should be holy and without blame before him in love: Having predestinated us unto the adoption of children by Jesus Christ to Himself, according to the good pleasure of His will."*
> *Ephesians 1:3-5*

● ● ●

The same anointing that abides in Him also abides in you.

● ● ●

You are of the same bloodline as the Anointed One. You carry his name. Everything that He has, He has also given to you. Just because you feel you were not favored with some special talent or amazing gift does not mean that you are not anointed. The Bible tells this amazing prophecy of what the anointing was going to do in the last days:

"And it shall come to pass in the last days, saith God, I will pour out of my Spirit upon all flesh: and your sons and your daughters shall prophesy, and your young men shall see visions, and your old men shall dream dreams: And on my servants and on my handmaidens I will pour out in those days of my Spirit; and they shall prophesy."

Acts 2: 17, 18

No one was left out in this passage! All flesh includes everyone–no matter what your station in life. If you are a blood washed, child of God, you have access to the Anointed One, Jesus the Christ, the son of the living God! You can trust that the anointing is on the inside of you. It is our Father's will that we abide in and be confident in His anointing:

"But the anointing which you have received from Him abides in you, and you do not need that anyone teach you; but as the same anointing teaches you concerning all things, and is true, and is not a lie, and just as it has taught you, you will abide in Him."

1 John 2:27 (NKJV)

"Know ye not that ye are the temple of God, and that the Spirit of God dwelleth in you?"

1 Corinthians 3:17

You are anointed because you house the Anointed One within you! You have the potential of being used by God in any of the gifts of the Spirit when you house His Spirit, so quit thinking of yourself as ordinary. You are extraordinary!

Think about it. The God of the entire universe has His Spirit dwelling within you. That should make you want to shout with a voice of praise! I don't know about you, but it makes me feel exceptional! It makes me want to walk around with my head up high! What a precious gift He bestowed upon and in us! His anointing confirms my heritage in Christ Jesus. Knowing who you are in Him is not walking in pride. It simply means that you are conscious that the precious oil of the Holy Spirit is living within you. Knowing this important truth should compel you to always protect the place where the anointing abides–your body which is the temple of God.

● ● ●

Don't exchange the working of the anointing in you for any ungodly characteristic that does not glorify God.

● ● ●

You must choose not to allow anything to defile your temple! Satan will throw everything at you to attempt to cause contamination, condemnation and intimidation as you house God's precious gift. Don't fall for it. Don't exchange the working of the anointing in you for any ungodly characteristic that does not glorify God. Put aside anger, backbiting, murmuring, complaining, and every evil work that will hinder the flow of the anointing in your life. Know this. There is no substitution for the anointing! Jesus paid a dear price so that you and I could receive His precious gift. Echo Job's assertion that *"My righteousness I hold fast, and will not let it go."* (Job 27:6)

● ● ●

There is no substitution for the anointing!

● ● ●

How do you guard the anointing? Stay in the Word of God. Pray without ceasing. Confess the Word of God over your life and family and over every situation that you face. Listen to hear what He has to say. Obey whatever He speaks to you. Walk in love. Connect with a church that teaches God's Word so that your faith can grow. Continue in fellowship with other believers.

"And they continued stedfastly in the apostles' doctrine and fellowship, and in breaking of bread, and in prayers."

Acts 2:42

Continuing is crucial in growing in the things of God. You must continue to fellowship with other believers, so that when adverse circumstances come against you, you can have others who can encourage you and pray with you so that you can be strengthened in the trial. Don't forsake this very special component:

"Not forsaking the assembling of ourselves together, as the manner of some is; but exhorting one another: and so much the more, as ye see the day approaching."

Hebrews 25:10

"Exhort" in this passage means to urge, press, push, and encourage. Although you have the anointing within you, there will be days that you may feel like giving up. Satan is working overtime to "wear out the saints!" Fellowship with other believers gives you the impetus to press through to victory! Stay connected, and you will experience supernatural courage in your daily walk with God.

It is a distinct honor to house the Anointed One within. You abide in Him, and He abides in you. Be confident in Him. If you allow Him, He will take you to heights that far exceed what you can ask or think!

You are anointed!

• • •
Confession

I am anointed. I carry the Anointing within me. Because He dwells within me, the oil of God's anointing flows through every area of my life. It is an honor and a pleasure to have His presence in me. I will treasure this wonderful gift for the rest of my life. I will keep my temple Holy and will purposefully protect this sacred gift.

Ephesians 2:18-22 (NKJV)

For through Him we both have access by one Spirit to the Father. Now, therefore, you are no longer strangers and foreigners, but fellow citizens with the saints and members of the household of God, having been built on the foundation of the apostles and prophets, Jesus Christ Himself being the chief cornerstone, in whom the whole building, being fitted together, grows into a holy temple in the Lord, in whom you also are being built together for a dwelling place of God in the Spirit.

• • •

Chapter 5
You Are Free

I received a Christian comic strip recently via e-mail that depicted a prison guard and the governor standing at an open gate. The governor asked the guard why was all of the pardoned prisoners still there. The guard simply replied that they would not leave.

Imagine that.

Every once in a while I read in the news about a prisoner who was exonerated or who was pardoned by the governor. I've also heard of a number of prisoners who were absolved of all wrongdoing after DNA testing confirmed their innocence. There have been press conferences with released prisoners who expressed their gratitude for their new-found freedom and who commence to tell what they plan to do now that they have their lives back.

In addition, I've seen movies about a convicted felon whose conviction was overturned. One such movie that comes to mind is *Hurricane*, the story of a professional boxer who was wrongly convicted of murder and locked away for life. Denzel Washington portrays the lead character that fought tirelessly for his freedom--all the while affirming his innocence. When he was finally released from prison after winning an appeal, he was elated to leave the bondage to which he had been subject to for over 20 years!

In all these examples, none of them turned down the opportunity to be free.

We were also set free from the bondage of sin. Jesus became sin for us and took our place on the cross of Calvary. He redeemed us from every curse of the law–which included hell, sickness and poverty. Because He took our place, we have been pardoned and set free forever! His promise to us was: *"If the Son therefore shall make you free, ye shall be free indeed."* You are completely free in Him!

Once the chains have been broken in your life, there is no need to look back. The comic strip reminded me of the children of Israel. After being set free by Pharoah and then witnessing the mighty and miraculous destruction of Pharoah's entire army, the children of Israel still thought it would be better to be back in Egypt (in bondage) than to wander in the desert (because of their disobedience I might add). They argued that at least in Egypt they had more of a variety to eat and plenty to drink. In the desert, they had to depend on God for everything. You would think that after seeing what He had already done for them, they would be confident that He would and could do for them exactly what He said He would do.

• • •

The children of Israel didn't realize how close they were to the promise because they kept looking back to the bondage!

• • •

The children of Israel didn't realize how close they were to the promise because they kept looking back to the bondage! Thomas Edison's famous quote resonates within as I think about the children of Israel: "Many of life's failures are people who did not realize how close they were to success when they gave up." Don't settle for the bondage of your past. The true you is free. You're free to live in victory. You're free to live in peace. You're free to live in abundance.

The enemy paints a very tempting picture of the past. The picture is just an illusion or a false impression that appears real. Just like the children of Israel, he wants to lure you back to slavery. He will pull out all the stops and use anyone who will allow him entrance to entice you to believe a LIE regarding your salvation or whatever situation you're dealing with. Returning to bondage is not the proper way to deal with temporary conditions.

● ● ●

Returning to bondage is not the proper way to deal with temporary conditions.

● ● ●

I've heard others state that people who do not confess Jesus were more of a blessing during some particularly tough periods in their life than their Christian sisters and brothers. I've even felt that way a time or two in my own life. During these emotionally draining moments, all of hell seems to come at you. The enemy knows that you are weak and vulnerable, so he cunningly "suggests" to you that living for Christ is not beneficial to you, and that you should quit church, quit the fellowship with other believers, and you will be better off without them.

Satan wants to isolate you and then bombard you with loneliness. He wants you to dwell on what life was like before you came to Christ, but remember, it will always be a distorted picture. He wants you to denounce Christ and anything associated with Him. He wants to lead you back to bondage, or if you're already in bondage, he wants to ensure that you remain there.

Don't do it. It's a trap. What looks like freedom is really entrapment and enslavement. Satan has nothing good to offer you, and his ultimate goal is to kill, steal and destroy. We must realize that we are to put our total trust and dependence in God.

Because of our humanness, we tend to let each other down.

"But we have this treasure in earthen vessels, that the excellency of the power may be of God, and not of us."

2 Corinthians 4:7

We're all still confined to earthen bodies. Because we may all be in different stages of our new life in Christ, we may not get it all right. In other words, we're not perfect. We all have sinned and come short of the glory of God. The beauty of salvation is that we can come boldly to the throne of grace, and God will meet us where we are.

When we look to others and they can't help us, don't be disappointed. God wants us to trust only Him. He never fails. He will never leave you nor forsake you. He wants to ensure that you remain free in Him. You are free from the ravages of sin and death. You can live in total freedom as you totally rely on our Father.

One of the benefits of freedom is growth and prosperity.

"Beloved, I wish above all things that thou mayest prosper and be in health, even as thy soul prospers."

3 John 2

To prosper means to flourish, to thrive or to grow. How can you grow if you are not free? Nothing that is in bondage can grow *properly* past the point of restriction!

• • •
Nothing that is in bondage can grow past the point of restriction!
• • •

For example, when my son, Joel, was born, he had an extended stay in the hospital because he was born prematurely. Upon his arrival, an identification band with his personal information was placed securely around his tiny ankle. His growth in the two months he was in the hospital was a very slow process, so none of us noticed that he was actually outgrowing his identification band! Before we knew it, the band was becoming extremely tight and had to be removed so as not to impede his growth process.

Do you get it? You must remain free in order to grow properly! You cannot be bound by chains of insecurity and inadequacy and live the life of victory that God has planned for you. Bondage will stop you cold from ever growing and maximizing your full potential and will ultimately keep you from your God-given destiny and the prosperity that Jesus died for you to have.

• • •

You cannot be bound by chains of insecurity and inadequacy and live the life of victory that God has planned for you.

• • •

Bondage wreaks havoc in many ways. It restrains you from moving forward with that new idea or invention. It keeps you from communicating with the person who holds some valuable information that could help you get to the next level. It suppresses you from starting that business or ministry. It hinders you from writing that book or launching your singing career. It inhibits you from reaching out to a long, lost relative or friend.

It is important to know that bondage does not always start out looking like bondage. In the case of my son, Joel, the identification band was for his own protection and for the protection of the hospital. It identified him as my son and also served as confirmation to the nurses that he was indeed the patient that should receive specific medications. As his tiny frame began to develop, however, the article that began as a good thing quickly became a not-so-good thing. If the band had not been removed, it would have eventually obstructed the circulation of blood in his leg. Not only could it have been a growth retardant, it could eventually cost him his life!

Do you see how important it is to be free? Joel's ID band is a natural example of how bondage can stunt your growth and lead to death. When we're in bondage in our minds, it blocks us from hearing the life-giving, supernatural words of deliverance from God. If we allow this condition to remain, it will eventually cause spiritual stagnation then death. Death simply means you can no longer "hear" God nor can you receive from Him. At this point you're just like a criminal in a cell; your cell happens to be in your mind.

• • •

Anything that is preventing you from growing or prospering is bondage

• • •

It is vital that we discern when something has outgrown its purpose and begins to put a stranglehold on us. How can you identify if you are in a bondage situation? Anything that obstructs your view or immobilizes you is bondage. Anything that causes undue fear in you is bondage. Sin is bondage.

Do not be concerned about what you will have to pay for this release from bondage. It's already been paid! Jesus paid for it with His life. If you will but embrace it, you can be eternally free! Don't stay in prison. Walk through the gate. Don't look back.

Recently, as I was listening to one of my favorite local radio stations, I heard a message that was so simple yet so amazingly profound. The station often plays motivational messages throughout the day. I love the messages, as they are presented with simplicity, which enhances its effectiveness in reaching those who may be apprehensive about establishing a relationship with Christ.

The message that caught my attention was about the debt of sin that we had accumulated over the years. The commentator used the example of someone who has a lifetime of credit card bills that he could never earn enough money to repay on an average salary. Nevertheless, Christ redeemed us by purchasing our debt for us with his death on the cross. You don't have to make restitution. You don't have to serve a certain amount of time in bondage here on earth to make up for the sins of your past. The Bible says that as far as the east is from the west, so far has he removed our transgressions from us. We are free!

God desired so much for us to live an abundant life on earth and to be free in Him that He gave His only Son. I admonish you to not let His sacrifice be in vain. He will never force Himself on you. He wants you to freely choose Him and all the benefits that come with living for Him.

> *"I call heaven and earth to record this day against you, that I have set before you life and death, blessing and cursing: therefore choose life, that both thou and thy seed may live."*
>
> *Deuteronomy 30:19*

If there ever was a scripture that we should pay attention to, it is this passage. God set before us two choices. Each one of them has a corresponding consequence. Cursing results in death. Blessing results in life. Life equals freedom. Death equals bondage. If these two choices don't shake you up, the follow-up to these choices should–*that both you and thy seed may live.* Your choice affects your children. I don't believe anyone wants their children to be effected by death and cursing–so choose life! Your children are depending on you!

Early in our marriage, my husband and I had a disagreement, and one of us was bitter (I believe it was me!). The Holy Spirit spoke so clearly to me that I was immediately compelled to change. He said that I had a choice. I could choose to be angry or to be forgiving. I chose to be forgiving.

There is always a choice: to obey or disobey; to lie or tell the truth; to be gracious or hateful. Just remember that the negative choices bring with them a harvest of death and cursing. The positive choices bring life and blessing. Life and blessing flows out of freedom in Jesus Christ.

You are free!

• • •

Confession

I am free! I am no longer bound by darkness. I no longer have shackles binding me. I have been set free from the bondage of sin and its effects that hinder my growth. From this day forward, I live a joyous and purposeful life. I am no longer bound by depression, shame, hurt, disappointment, misery and defeat. I now live a life of blessings, contentment, joy, peace and freedom. Today, I choose life!

John 10:10

The thief cometh not, but for to steal, and to kill, and to destroy: I am come that they might have life, and that they might have it more abundantly.

• • •

Chapter 6
You Are Blessed

That's the truth. You are blessed! Not because I said it. The Word of God declares it! If you don't quite believe me, let's look at this powerful passage of Scripture:

"And it shall come to pass, if thou shalt hearken diligently unto the voice of the Lord thy God, to observe and do all His commandments which I command thee this day, that the Lord thy God will set thee on high above all nations of the earth.

And all these blessings shall come on thee, and overtake thee, if thou shalt hearken unto the voice of the Lord thy God.

Blessed shalt thou be in the city, and blessed shalt thou be in the field.

Blessed shall be the fruit of thy body, and the fruit of thy ground, and the fruit of thy cattle, the increase of thy kine, and the flocks of thy sheep.

Blessed shall be thy basket and thy store.

Blessed shalt thou be when thou comest in, and blessed shalt thou be when thou goest out.

The Lord shall cause thine enemies that rise up against thee to be smitten before thy face: they shall come against thee one way, and flee before thee seven ways.

The Lord shall command the blessing upon thee in thy storehouses, and in all that thou settest thine hand unto; and He shall bless thee in the land which the Lord thy God giveth thee."

Deuteronomy 28:1-8

And these are just the first eight verses! There are more blessings in verses 9-13. Do you see how many blessings are in this passage?

Isn't it amazing that so many of us have not tapped into these awesome blessings that God has given us? Sometimes we think that just because things are not going our way that we aren't blessed. When we focus for too long on the adverse circumstances, then comes the evil one and tells us the opposite of what God says in these verses. Satan immediately comes to steal the Word from us, and if we capitulate, we begin a vicious cycle of negative thinking and exhibit what Hebrews describes as "an evil heart of unbelief." Satan laughs when we're in this state, because he knows that he has stolen the benefits that are ours.

● ● ●

Don't focus on where you are. Focus on where you want to be.

● ● ●

One thing that God said for us not to forget is His benefits. God says in His Word that every need that we have is met. We all have lean times in our lives, but if we focus on what our Father said and continue to trust that He cannot lie, we will eventually experience the harvest that He has for us.

Don't focus on where you are. Focus on where you want

to be! Get a God-sized vision. Call those things that be not as though they were. God is the one who gives us power to get wealth so that He might establish His covenant. If we keep the proper perspective that wealth is not so that we can consume it on ourselves but that it is to be used for the purposes of God, we will position ourselves for His blessings to flow to and through us.

What is so key here is that we believe what God says. He says He gives us the power to get wealth. Power in the Hebrew means ability, substance and strength. If you look at your checkbook and it registers below the poverty level, it's time to draw upon God's wisdom to change that condition. If you're sick, and Jesus says that by His stripes you are healed, it's time to speak healing over your body. God says you're blessed! If your circumstances don't say blessed, stand in faith until your circumstances change. Rejoice in whatever circumstance in which you find yourself. God always has a way of escape, because He wants to pour out His blessings upon you.

Paul said, *"Actually, I don't have a sense of needing anything personally. I've learned by now to be quite content whatever my circumstances. I'm just as happy with little as with much, with much as with little."* (Philippians 4:11, The Message)

● ● ●

We're not just survivors. We are more than conquerors!

● ● ●

Many read this passage of scripture and immediately surmise that whatever is happening to me is my lot in life. I don't have to have much. I can just survive, and I'll be okay. That is not God's best for us. We're not just survivors. We are more than conquerors! Paul was simply saying that even though my circumstances may sometimes be challenging, I can still be content. I can still rejoice because greater is He that is in me than he that is in the world. I can be content because circumstances are temporary. Seasons do change. It is our job to stand until we receive breakthrough. Don't give up before breakthrough!

Paul further stated, *"But my God shall supply all your need according to His riches in glory by Christ Jesus."* (Philippians 4:19). Please note that He (God) supplies your need according to His riches. Wouldn't you say that our Father is very rich? If He made all the worlds and everything in it, I would say He has lots of wealth. Not only does He have wealth, He says to the person that greatly fears Him, *"wealth and riches shall be in his house."* (Psalm 112:3). Wealth is not only money. He gives us a wealth of wisdom, knowledge, influence, peace, joy, etc. He meant for us to be perfectly whole in every area of our life. But we must contend for it.

Throughout the Word of God we have found example after example that He is the God of more than enough. If you're blessed coming in and going out, we're not talking lack. If God commands His blessing on you, who can stop it? The answer is you. He wants you to walk in faith. He wants you to believe Him when He tells you that you're blessed. Let's give further examples of what it means to be blessed.

Blessed means you don't have to be unduly concerned about what is going on around you. *"A thousand shall fall at thy side, and ten thousand at thy right hand; but it shall not come nigh thee."* (Psalm 91:7). Why? Because you're blessed. Blessed means you're surrounded with God's favor. Blessed means that when you encounter challenges, you can look at the situation through the eyes of the Spirit and discern that there is a treasure to be gotten from it:

"And I will give thee the treasures of darkness, and hidden riches of secret places, that thou mayest know that I, the Lord, which call thee by thy name, am the God of Israel."

Isaiah 45:3

Blessed means you can cast all your cares on our Father, and He will strengthen, uphold and help you. Get the picture? Blessed is the opposite of cursed. Satan ushered in the curse.

You do not have to accept it. You may ask in your mind, "How can I know in my heart that I'm blessed?" Glad you asked. Paul in his letter to the Romans gave an excellent exhortation:

"And be not conformed to this world: but be ye transformed by the renewing of your mind..."

Romans 12:2

To renew your mind, you must meditate the Word of God until it takes root in the fertile soil of your heart. Spend time praying in the Spirit and speaking forth God's promises. Before you realize it, you'll be walking and talking with boldness and confidence, and nothing will be able to shake you. As you daily renew your mind, what used to make you nervous and afraid will no longer have power over you. That's the blessing becoming evident in you. People will stand up and take notice that you are indeed blessed!

Now remember that being blessed also means empowerment. God gave us power to get wealth. That means some work is involved. It would be nice if God just rained wealth out of heaven–but that's not His way. All the wealth we need is right here on earth. He supplies the wisdom and opportunities, and we must be able to discern when opportunity knocks at the door. One of the famous quotes attributed to Thomas Edison is "opportunity is missed by most people, because it is dressed in overalls and looks like work."

Now get this. We are blessed to work. Work was instituted in the Garden of Eden before Satan showed up. Work helps us to be able to solve problems for others, take care of our families, and to take the message of salvation to the marketplace. Work provides us with seeds to sow in the kingdom of God. God has a purpose for everything that He created and for everything He asked us to do. Everything God created is a blessing.

Begin to think with the mind of Christ: *"For as he thinketh in his heart, so is he."* (Prov. 23:7). Allow the transforming power of God's Word to do its perfect work, and you will begin to see who *the true you* really are! When you begin to see through the eyes of the Spirit, it won't matter what you see with your natural eyes. If you can see it, you can change it. It's your perception that has to change. When you begin to think biblically, you can create, map out and design a bountiful life in Him! It doesn't matter what you have or don't have now. Just begin to believe the benefits God says are yours.

Have you seen people who are very successful? There's something about them that makes you look at them again and again. They walk differently. They talk differently. They even think differently. You won't hear them saying why they can't. You will hear them saying how they can. They don't respond to every negative thing said against them. They don't have time. They are focused on what they're to accomplish. They don't embrace the status quo. They are independent thinkers who push aside every obstacle and push through to what they have already seen.

• • •

Blessings only come on you and overtake you when you follow hard after Christ by doing the things He said to do.

• • •

If people who are not necessarily God chasers can have a vision and see it through to fruition, surely God's people, who have already been given the blessing, can do the same! Don't run with the turkeys! Only hang out with the eagles! *Mark the perfect man*, the Bible states. Find people who are where you're trying to be, and begin to get the wealth of knowledge and wisdom that God has in them for you. Remember, it's a part of the blessing! Blessings only come on you and overtake you when you follow hard after Christ by doing the things He said to do. That's why fellowship with Him is so important. As you seek His face, He'll tell you His heart. The blessing will then come on you and overtake you!

To stay in the flow of blessing, keep (guard) your heart with all diligence. What you allow in your heart will flow out into every area of your life. If you allow negative people to continually speak into your life, it will eventually take root, and you will reap a harvest that you don't desire. *"But shun profane and vain babblings: for they will increase unto more ungodliness."* (2 Tim. 2:16). When people see that you don't participate in their negativity, it may burn up your "cool" card, but they will respect you in the long run. Keep the blessings operating in your life. If you have corrupt seeds planted in your heart, confess it to God, and uproot them. Don't allow them to grow any longer. You shall bring forth good fruit. No corrupt fruit here!

> • • •
> To stay in the flow of blessing, keep (guard) your heart with all diligence. What you allow in your heart will flow out into every area of your life.
> • • •

I love being blessed. I do whatever is necessary to keep myself in its flow. I'm diligent about what I allow in my thoughts. Just as I fiercely protect my children and my relationship with my husband, I fiercely protect my heart. I guard my heart by continually feeding my spirit with the Word of God. I often refer to the passage in Deuteronomy which details the blessings that I am entitled to receive as a believer. I identify with the blessings and not with the circumstances I may be currently in. As a child of God, I'm supposed to get my identity from Him, and if He says I'm blessed, then bless God I'm blessed!

As I grew up in church, I often wondered why when you asked a Christian how they were doing; they would respond that they were "blessed." Whether they were aware of it or not, they were creating in the spirit realm the harvest of blessing! God is Creator, and we were made in His image. If He could create, then we can create! He said "let there be", and there was. He's given us the same creative ability. That's why it's important what you say. Let's look at the following passage:

"As it is written, I have made thee a father of many nations before Him whom he believed, even God, who quickeneth the dead, and calleth those things which be not as though they were.

Who against hope, believed in hope, that he might become the father of many nations, according to that which was spoken, So shall thy seed be.

And being not weak in faith, he considered not his own body now dead, when he was about an hundred years old, neither yet the deadness of Sarah's womb.

He staggered not at the promise of God through unbelief; but was strong in faith, giving glory to God;

And being fully persuaded that, what He had promised, he was able also to perform."

Romans 4:17-21

Now that is what I call walking in the blessing! Here's a man, Abraham, 100 years old, and still confessing that he's the father of many nations. He has not yet had any children, his wife is 90 years old, and she has never had any children. Yet this passage says that he neither considered his body nor Sarah's dead womb. The Greek definition for "consider" is to observe fully; to perceive. In other words, he didn't even add his body into the equation. He relied totally on the Word that was spoken to him by God! It further says that Abraham did not stagger in unbelief. He was not believing one minute and disbelieving the next. When there should have been no reason to hope, he kept right on hoping–believing the spoken Word of God.

If Abraham, who was under the old covenant, could believe God, then we are without excuse. What was an impossible situation in the natural was made possible by believing what God said, speaking what God said, and standing until it manifested. It is the same pattern we are to use today. As we stand in faith, we bring glory to God! The truth of God's Word will supersede your circumstances every time. Jesus said, "I am the truth."

Choose to believe the truth of God's Word that you are blessed! As you continue to stand on that truth, your faith will soar to heights that you had never known. The blessings will be evident for all to see, and you will be a blessing!

You are blessed!

• • •

Confession

I am blessed! God's Word says that I'm blessed in the city and the fields. Everywhere I go, I'm blessed. When the sun rises and sets, I'm blessed. Despite what may be happening in my life, I'm blessed. I will rest in the truth of God's Word. I will not waiver in unbelief. I will hold fast to His promises.

Psalm 84:12

O Lord of Hosts, blessed is the man that trusteth in thee.

• • •

Chapter 7
You Are Royalty

I love a good rags-to-riches story. In The Pursuit of Happyness, Will Smith plays the character of Chris Gardner, a struggling, and eventually homeless, San Francisco salesman who is left to raise his five-year-old son, Christopher, on a next-to-nothing salary. Against extreme odds and through sweat, determination and a wonderful break through an acquaintance, he achieves the pinnacle of success as a stock broker. It warms the heart that Mr. Gardner's experiences culminated in a wonderful ending.

Then there are some of us who also experienced various forms of poverty–until we were reborn into the kingdom of God. This is the ultimate rags-to-riches story. When we accepted Jesus as Savior, we became part of a royal priesthood!

> *"But ye are a chosen generation, a royal priesthood, an holy nation, a peculiar people; that ye should shew forth the praises of him who hath called you out of darkness into His marvelous light."*
>
> *1 Peter 2:9*

Just as Christopher stands to inherit his father's fortune, we will also inherit our Father's riches. Every benefit that is His belongs to us! We were supernaturally adopted into a royal family. Because we're joint heirs with Jesus Christ, we inherited an abundant life on earth, and we will also inherit a glorious life in heaven!

I desired to learn more about what an inheritance meant, so I searched the book that is an expert on inheritance–the Bible. I found that there were more than 200 scripture references about inheritances. I noted that the majority of them were in the Old Testament. God was big into inheritance, so when he began to speak to Abram, the first thing He said to him was to leave his country and his comfort zone. Abram needed preparation for where he was going and for what he was about to inherit.

When you are about to inherit immense wealth in the natural, you need people around you who can counsel and prepare you for handling it if you've never experienced wealth. If you don't prepare, you will ultimately lose it. What God was about to do through Abram was totally off the charts! This is the promise that God made to Abram:

> *"And I will make of thee a great nation, and I will bless thee, and make thy name great; and thou shalt be a blessing.*
>
> *And I will bless them that bless thee, and curse him that curseth thee: and in thee shall all families of the earth be blessed."*
>
> *Genesis 12:2, 3*

This is where it really begins to get exciting for us as believers. Not only is God promising to bless and make of Abram a great nation, but in him shall all families of the earth be blessed. That's you and me! Hallelujah! Each time God visited Abram, He repeated the blessing over him and Abram built an altar and worshiped God. There seems to be a pattern here. God visits, you're blessed and you worship. Here's another nugget that we will see in this next passage:

"And the Lord said unto Abram, after that Lot was separated from him. Lift up now thine eyes, and look from the place where thou art northward, and southward, and eastward and westward.

For all the land which thou seest, to thee will I give it, and to thy seed forever.

And I will make thy seed as the dust of the earth: so that if a man can number the dust of the earth, then shall thy seed also be numbered.

Arise, walk through the land in the length of it and in the breadth of it; for I will give it unto thee."

Genesis 13:14-17

God knows how important it is for us to see as well as hear His promise to us. God told Abram to look everywhere, and whatever he could see, that's what He was going to give to him. He also told Abram to walk the length and breadth of the land, because He was going to give it to him. In further passages, the Lord told Abram to look at the heavens and the stars. Just as you can't number the stars, the Lord said that Abram's seed could not be numbered.

• • •

God knows how important it is for us to see as well as hear His promise to us.

• • •

What the Lord is drawing forth from Abram is his creative abilities. God *saw* the earth *before* he spoke it into existence. Abram was encouraged to imagine all the promises of God as well as speak the promises of God. That's another pattern for us if we are to benefit from being a royal priesthood.

After 15 years upon leaving Ur of the Chaldees, Abram was now 90 years old. God continues to remind him of His promise to him. It's about to get glorious now! God changes Abram's name to Abraham which means "father of many nations." How cool is that! Now every time someone spoke his name, they were "calling those things that be not as though they were!" God wanted to instill into Abraham who the true him was! He was preparing to walk into his inheritance!

So what actually is an inheritance? An inheritance is the right of an heir to assume ownership of wealth or a title when an ancestor dies. In the Old Testament, an inheritance was automatically assumed by the first-born son upon his father's death. Each first-born son inherited their father's wealth, legacy and title. Because God instituted this line of succession, His covenant was the first ever written will and testament. Once put into effect, it was automatically based upon the order of birth.

An inheritance protected the stability of the family. A family's inheritance did not transfer across tribal or blood lines. God's people were expected to leave an inheritance even to their children's children. (Prov. 13:22). The act of building and maintaining an inheritance was just as scriptural and spiritual as "loving your neighbor as yourself."

A particular passage of scripture came to mind as I pondered over the concept of inheritance. The story of Jacob and Esau in Genesis, Chapters 25 and 27 demonstrates inheritance in a very dramatic way. Jacob and Esau were twin brothers, who were born to Isaac and Rebekah. While Rebekah had them in her womb, the Bible says they struggled together. Rebekah didn't understand it, so she asked God why this was happening. The Lord replied that there were two nations in her, and two sets of people would come from her. One would be stronger than the other, and the elder would serve the younger.

What's notable about this story is that when they were being born, Esau was born first, but when Jacob came out, he grabbed Esau's heel. That was the second phenomenon concerning the twins. As Jacob and Esau grew, Esau became a clever hunter while Jacob was a plain (gentle or pious) man. Isaac favored Esau while Rebekah favored Jacob. Being a man's man, Isaac probably favored Esau because he was the first-born and also because he exhibited more strength and ability than Jacob. Isaac also enjoyed the wonderful cooked venison from Esau's hunting. Jacob, on the other hand, probably stimulated his mother's feminine side because he was so gentle. For whatever reason, they each favored one son over the other.

What happened next was life-changing to the entire family. Esau came in from hunting and was very tired and hungry. The last thing he wanted to do was cook! Jacob had already cooked lentils, so Esau asked for some. Jacob must have been looking for an opportunity for a long time to gain Esau's inheritance, and he discerned that this was it. Instead of a simple yes, Jacob said *"sell me this day thy birthright."* What? Esau became incensed and retorted that he was about to die, and his birthright didn't account for anything at the moment. However, Jacob persisted and made Esau swear that he would sell him his birthright–for a bowl of food! What is so incredulous is that Esau accepted Jacob's offer–just because he was hungry! The inheritance that should have gone to Esau from his father, Isaac, was sold for a mere bowl of vegetables and some bread. The Bible records that *"Esau despised his birthright."* "Despised" here means he lightly esteemed his birthright.

The story grows even more interesting. When Isaac had gotten old and almost blind, he called his eldest son to him. When Isaac asked Esau to hunt for venison, prepare it and bring it to him so he could eat, he added that he was going to bless Esau–a momentous occasion in the life of a Hebrew. This blessing entailed bestowing upon him his inheritance as the first-born son.

Meanwhile, Rebekah heard the exchange between Isaac and Esau and immediately went to look for Jacob. She repeated to Jacob what Isaac said to Esau. She then asked Jacob to go get two young goats. She planned to make the meat just like Isaac loved it and pass off Jacob as if he were Esau. Jacob would get the inheritance, and Esau would not. Jacob was very concerned about the deception and was afraid his father would discover he was not Esau and would curse him instead of bless him. Jacob reminded his mother that Esau was hairy, and he was not. In other words, I won't be able to fool dad!

However, Rebekah has thought this through, and she has a plan. Jacob returns with the goats, and Rebekah hurriedly prepares the dish just as Isaac likes it. She then gets Esau's clothes and put them on Jacob. She also applies the skin of the goats on his hands and on his neck. She then gave Jacob the meat to take to his father.

When Jacob approached his father, the first clue that something was not quite right was that it should have taken longer to hunt the meat and then cook it. Isaac asked Jacob how could he have hunted and prepared it so quickly to which Jacob replied, *"The Lord thy God brought it to me."* The second clue was that Jacob didn't sound like Esau, so Isaac asked him to come closer so *"that I may feel thee, my son, whether thou be my very son Esau or not."* So Jacob came closer, and Isaac began to feel his hands, and they were indeed hairy like Esau's hands. The scripture says, *"And he discerned him not, because his hands were hairy as his brother Esau's hands: so he blessed him."*

• • •

Isaac continued to be troubled by what his heart knew as opposed to what his flesh confirmed.

• • •

Isaac continued to be troubled by what his heart knew as opposed to what his flesh confirmed. (That statement could lead to an entirely different message, but I will continue to affirm your royal line!)

He again asked Jacob, *"Art thou my very son, Esau?"* And Jacob said, *"I am."* Jacob was given multiple opportunities to recant his deception, but he chose to follow through with the lie. At the beginning of the story, the Lord told Rebekah while the boys were yet in her womb that the elder would serve the younger. Instead of waiting for God's plan to unfold His way, she took the situation into her hands and made a royal mess.

After Isaac ate and drank with Jacob, he commenced to bless him. He appears to still be troubled that something was not quite right about Jacob. He smelled Jacob's clothes, and because they smelled like Esau's clothes, he settled down in his mind that he was indeed Esau. Here is where Isaac gives the first-born blessing:

> *"And he came near, and kissed him: and he smelled the smell of his raiment, and blessed him, and said, See, the smell of my son is as the smell of a field which the Lord hath blessed:*
>
> *Therefore God give thee of the dew of heaven, and the fatness of the earth, and plenty of corn and wine:*
>
> *Let people serve thee, and nations bow down to thee: be Lord over thy brethren, and let thy mother's sons bow down to thee: cursed be every one that curseth thee, and blessed be he that blessed thee."*
>
> *Genesis 27:27-29*

Now as soon as Isaac blessed Jacob, in came Esau. His inheritance had just slipped through his fingers, and he was about to find that out.

> *"And it came to pass, as soon as Isaac had made an end of blessing Jacob, and Jacob was scarce gone out from the presence of Isaac, his father, that Esau his brother came in from his hunting.*
>
> *And he also had made savoury meat, and brought it unto his father, and said unto his father, Let my father arise, and eat of his son's venison, that thy soul may bless me.*

And Isaac his father said unto him, Who art thou? And he said, I am thy son, thy firstborn Esau.

And Isaac trembled very exceedingly, and said, Who? where is he that hath taken venison, and brought it to me, and I have eaten of all before thou camest, and have blessed him? yea, and he shall be blessed.

And when Esau heard the words of his father, he cried with a great and exceeding bitter cry, and said unto his father, Bless me, even me also, O my father.

And he said, Thy brother came with subtilty, and hath taken away thy blessing.

And he said, Is not he rightly named Jacob? for he hath supplanted me these two times: he took away my birthright; and, behold, now he hath taken away my blessing. And he said, Hast thou not reserved a blessing for me?

And Isaac answered and said unto Esau, Behold, I have made him thy lord, and all his brethren have I given to him for servants; and with corn and wine have I sustained him: and what shall I do now unto thee, my son?

And Esau said unto his father, Hast thou but one blessing, my father? bless me, even me also, O my father. And Esau lifted up his voice, and wept

And Isaac his father answered and said unto him, Behold, thy dwelling shall be the fatness of the earth, and of the dew of heaven from above;

And by thy sword shalt thou live, and shalt serve thy brother; and it shall come to pass when thou shalt have the dominion, that thou shalt break his yoke from off thy neck.

And Esau hated Jacob because of the blessing wherewith his father blessed him: and Esau said in his heart, The days of mourning for my father are at hand; then will I slay my brother Jacob."

Genesis 27:30-41

Rebekah and Jacob went to extreme measures to deceive Isaac. Isaac's blessing was the equivalent of our present-day will. It was legal and binding. The blessing was spoken over Jacob, and it could not be retracted. There was something spiritual released into the atmosphere when these blessings were spoken. Esau understood this and was full of anguish and hatred for his brother. And you think you have a dysfunctional family! Jacob stood to inherit everything. Let's take a look at the great wealth that Isaac had.

"Then Isaac sowed in that land, and received in the same year an hundredfold: and the Lord blessed him.

And the man waxed great, and went forward, and grew until he became very great:

For he had possession of flocks, and possession of herds, and great store of servants: and the Philistines envied him."

Not only did Isaac pass to Jacob the wealth that he acquired through hard work and God's blessings but also the wealth that he inherited from his father:

And Abraham gave all that he had to Isaac."

Genesis 25:5

Whew! As you can see, inheritance was not taken lightly. You can see God's sentiments regarding inheritance in this strong statement:

"As it is written, Jacob have I loved, but Esau have I hated."

Romans 9:13

What? Why would God hate Esau when Jacob was the one who was deceitful? Because Esau despised his birthright. He esteemed very lightly the spiritual legacy that God instituted. He gave away his inheritance and all that it entailed for a mere bowl of food.

• • •
Don't esteem lightly your inheritance as a king and priest!
• • •

What is the great lesson here? We return to the title of this chapter. You are royalty. Don't take lightly your royal status that God has bestowed upon you! If God says you're a royal priesthood, then act like it! Don't esteem lightly your inheritance as a king and priest! Don't accept what some demon spirit says to you! He only wants to rob you of your inheritance! What belongs to Christ also belongs to you. When you become royalty, your cultural status changes. You're no longer a mere man. You're seated in heavenly places with Christ! Hallelujah!

Isaac was so blessed that Abimilech said to him, *"Go from us; for thou art much mightier than we."* (Genesis 26:16). David echoes this in Psalm 112:2 when referring to God's offspring that fear Him: *"His seed shall be mighty upon earth; the generation of the upright shall be blessed."* There it is again! Your seed represents your heirs. Maintain your royal status so that whoever succeeds you will step right into your royal position!

If God thought enough of us to make a will (covenant) with us, surely we should do the same–naturally and spiritually. What is the first thing you want to know when you learn you're in someone's will? You want to know, "what do I stand to inherit?" In order to learn what's in the will, someone has to read it. That's why God told Moses:

"And ye shall teach your children, speaking to them when thou sittest in thine house, and when thou walkest by the way, when thou liest down, and when thou risest up."

Deuteronomy 11:19

In other words, be sure that your children know what is in the will. If you don't read the will, you won't know your benefits. God said not to forget His benefits! One of the benefits that I found in God's Will and Testament is that *"I will be a crown of glory in the hand of the Lord, and a royal diadem in the hand of my God."* (Isaiah 62:3). I'm royalty! And so are you!

A present-day example of royalty is the British monarchy. The lines of succession are clearly drawn. When the present reigning person dies, there is no meeting to decide who will ascend the throne. It is according to birth. So it is with every child of God.

Paul, as a Hebrew, understood what it meant to have an inheritance. When speaking of the Lord Jesus he stated:

"In whom also we have obtained an inheritance, being predestined according to the purpose of him who works all things according to the counsel of his will."

Ephesians 1:11 (NKJV)

"He saved us, not because of righteous things we had done, but because of His mercy. He saved us through the washing of rebirth and renewal by the Holy Spirit, whom he poured out on us generously through Jesus Christ our Savior, so that, having been justified by his grace, we might become heirs having the hope of eternal life."

Titus 3:5-7(NLT)

Our inheritance was obtained through our rebirth. We were branches of a wild olive tree, but now we are grafted into a good olive tree. We receive our nourishment from the good tree's root and fatness. (Romans 11:17). In other words, we were adopted as sons and daughters of our heavenly Father.

Someone had to die before we could receive our inheritance. Jesus volunteered to redeem man back to God, and His shed blood alone gave us the right to every blessing and benefit that are for God's children. Because of the blood, we are now part of the blood line of Christ, and we have every right to claim our inheritance as royalty. Because Prince Charles was born into the British royal family, he has access to wealth, education and status that others could never have. Apart from Jesus, we would have never had access to the kingdom. Now we are joint heirs!

In the natural, an inheritance could be lost, broken, squandered or lose value–according to what is inherited. In the kingdom of God, we have *"an inheritance incorruptible, and undefiled, and that fadeth not away, which is reserved in heaven."* (1 Peter 1:4). What an inheritance!

You are heirs to our majesty Father's throne. You're part of a royal lineage. Don't despise it. Worship God. Maintain your inheritance. Continually remind your heirs about the Will and its benefits. Bask in the royalty that you are.

You are royalty!

• • •
Confession
I am royalty. I have been supernaturally adopted into a royal family by my faith in Jesus Christ. I will no longer accept a poverty mentality. I will embrace my royal status as a joint heir with Jesus Christ. I will live in earnest expectation of the blessings that I am destined to receive as a born-again believer.

Revelations 5:10
And hast made us unto our God kings and priests: and we shall reign on the earth.
• • •

Chapter 8
You Are Favored

Being popular, extremely talented and very attractive is at the top of the list for many people. Others desire prestigious positions and great power. There's nothing wrong with the desires if put into proper perspective. They could also provide entrance for you into many places, bring you before influential people and may also bring you great wealth. Nevertheless, I've found in my years on earth that one attribute that is often not recognized is favor.

• • •
To be favored means you're a recipient of someone's goodwill which manifests as a kind act.
• • •

Favor can be described many ways, but let's just look at a few of them. To be favored means you're a recipient of someone's goodwill which manifests as a kind act. Someone does something for you just because they want to. Favored also means you've been given grace. You didn't earn it. You were given a reprieve for something that was destined to happen to you–such as a stay of execution, a warning when you should have been given a traffic ticket, etc. In other words, mercy was bestowed on you. Job said it best in this passage:

"Thou hast granted me life and favor, and thy visitation hath preserved my spirit."

Job 12:2

Favor results in being chosen. If God were to pick someone for his team, he would choose you. You weren't chosen as an afterthought. He had you on his mind over 2,000 years ago! He prefers you. He approves of you. You're His favorite!

The Tour de France is an annual bicycle race that covers 2,200 miles around France. Lance Armstrong, the renowned cyclist who competed in this race, won first place a record shattering seven consecutive years. When Lance was in his prime, he was "favored" to win each time he competed. All eyes would be on him throughout the race. Everyone watched cycling's golden boy with high expectation. Lance's incredible stamina and determination was greatly admired. His participation and wins helped to attract many spectators to the sport. The constant media attention catapulted Lance to a level of superstardom that was on par with Hollywood's elite.

To many of his fans' delight, Lance announced his plans to race again in 2010. What is so extraordinary about his announcement is that he is now 38 years old (an advanced age in the world of sports); he has been on an extended break, which means he has not been training for some time; and he has recently recovered from testicular cancer which actually spread to his brain and his lungs. Though he may not be "favored" by the majority to win, he is still considered to be a worthy contender.

Just as the world is watching Lance, all of heaven is watching you and cheering you on. God Himself has favored you to win every time! He has great plans for you!

"For I know the thoughts that I think toward you, saith the Lord, thoughts of peace, and not of evil, to give you an expected end."

Jeremiah 29:11

God wants you to win. He prefers you. He approves of you. You may feel as if you're not in shape spiritually or that you don't qualify, but heaven and the world is watching you in this race called life.

Having the Lord's approval means much more to me than having anyone else's approval. Knowing that He is pleased with me and that He supports me is so precious to me. Knowing that I am in God's favor gives me courage to approach life with hope and excitement!

I once shared with my husband a business deal that I was considering. He listened very intensely, offered no negative feedback and responded with words of support and affirmation. In other words, he favored me with his encouragement. Likewise, our Father encourages us through His Word, through the Holy Spirit and through other believers. He gives us courage to face each day–knowing we walk in His favor.

As I prayed about what the Lord would have me say to you about His favor, I believe He wanted this chapter to affirm to you that He's in your corner. God's favor leads to life:

"...in His favor is life."

Psalm 30:5

God's favor is all around you.

"For thou, Lord, wilt bless the righteous; with favor wilt thou compass him as with a shield."

Psalm 5:12

Let's look at how favor is shown in this story:

"Now there was a certain man of Ramathaimzophim, of mount Ephraim, and his name was Elkanah, the son of Jeroham, the son of Elihu, the son of Tohu, the son of Zuph, an Ephrathite:

And he had two wives; the name of the one was

Hannah, and the name of the other Peninnah: and Peninnah had children, but Hannah had no children.

And this man went up out of his city yearly to worship and to sacrifice unto the Lord of hosts in Shiloh. And the two sons of Eli, Hophni and Phinehas, the priests of the Lord, were there.

And when the time was that Elkanah offered, he gave to Peninnah his wife, and to all her sons and her daughters, portions:

But unto Hannah he gave a worthy portion; for he loved Hannah: but the Lord had shut up her womb.

And her adversary also provoked her sore, for to make her fret, because the Lord had shut up her womb.

And as he did so year by year, when she went up to the house of the Lord, so she provoked her; therefore she wept, and did not eat.

Then said Elkanah her husband to her, Hannah, why weepest thou? and why eatest thou not? and why is thy heart grieved? am not I better to thee than ten sons?"

1 Samuel 1:1-8

Elkanah had two wives: Peninnah and Hannah. Peninnah was very fruitful. Hannah was barren. In that day, the ability to have children–especially a male child—was considered a blessing and not being able to have them was thought of as a curse. When Elkanah went to sacrifice at the temple, he gave both his wives and children portions of the meat, but he gave more to Hannah, for he loved Hannah. A man's status was greatly enhanced when he had many sons, and although Hannah wasn't able to give him sons, Elkanah still favored her. Elkanah loved Hannah unconditionally. Peninnah had his children, but Hannah had his heart.

● ● ●

His plans will lead to a victorious life in Him.

● ● ●

That was a snapshot of how God's favor works. We didn't do anything to earn it. He just loves and favors us! No matter what state you're in or what you have done, God prefers you. He has plans for you. His plans will lead to a victorious life in Him. Be strengthened, and know that you are favored!

• • •

Confession

My Father has plans for me. His favor is all around me. I walk in His favor. I can do all things through Christ as He strengthens and favors me!

Proverbs 8:35

For whoso findeth me findeth life, and shall obtain favor of the Lord.

• • •

Chapter 9
You Are Covered

The story of Noah and the ark is one that has been rehearsed throughout generations. In summary, God told Noah to build an ark to His exact specifications. God made Noah privy to His plans to destroy the earth and began to prepare Noah, his family and a male and female from every creature to be preserved.

Now, one of the things that is so significant about God's instructions is that what He told Noah would happen had never happened before. Rain had never come down from heaven, and what God was prophesying was a flood. (Genesis 2:5, 6). Once the ark was complete and Noah's family and the creatures were inside, God Himself locked the door, and then the rain came down.

God ensured that the ark's occupants were "covered" from destruction, while the earth was "uncovered" for destruction. You are protected and covered by God if you have given your life to Him. He covers you when you act on His Word. If Noah had not acted on what God said to Him–even though there was no precedent for a flood–Noah and his descendants and every animal would have been destroyed. There would have been no one or no thing left to reproduce and multiply.

There are numerous instances in the Bible where God covered His people:

> *"And of Benjamin he said, The beloved of the Lord shall dwell in safety by him; and the Lord shall cover him all the day long, and he shall dwell between his shoulders."*
>
> *Deuteronomy 33:12*

> *"He shall cover thee with His feathers, and under His wings shalt thou trust; His truth shall be thy shield and buckler."*
>
> *Psalm 91:4*

One of the most miraculous examples of God's covering was when He was preparing to liberate the children of Israel from Egypt:

> *"And the blood shall be to you for a token upon the houses where ye are: and when I see the blood, I will pass over you, and the plague shall not be upon you to destroy you, when I smite the land of Egypt."*
>
> *Exodus 12:13*

Covered by the blood! In God, you have security that cannot be replicated by man. He is the all-seeing, all-knowing God, so nothing is hid from Him. He knows all of Satan's traps assigned against you, and He secures you under His covering.

On the other hand, Satan's plan is to uncover you for destruction. Let's consider this passage from Genesis:

> *"And the sons of Noah, that went forth of the ark, were Shem, and Ham, and Japheth: and Ham is the father of Canaan.*

These are the sons of Noah: and of them was the whole earth overspread.

And Noah began to be an husbandman, and he planted a vineyard:

And he drank of the wine, and was drunken; and he was uncovered within his tent.

And Ham, the father of Canaan, saw the nakedness of his father, and told his two brethren without.

And Shem and Japheth took a garment, and laid it upon both their shoulders, and went backward, and covered the nakedness of their father; and their faces were backward, and they saw not their father's nakedness.

And Noah awoke from his wine, and knew what his younger son had done unto him.

And he said, Cursed be Canaan; a servant of servants shall he be unto his brethren.

And he said, Blessed be the Lord God of Shem; and Canaan shall be his servant.

God shall enlarge Japheth, and he shall dwell in the tents of Shem; and Canaan shall be his servant."

Genesis 9:18-27

Noah was drunk after drinking too much wine from his vineyard. For whatever reason, he was naked when Ham found him. He most likely passed out before he could get under the bed covers. Because Noah was drunk and uncovered, he was made vulnerable to whoever saw him. His guard was down, and he risked exposure in his weakened state. He was susceptible to physical and spiritual danger.

Ham was amused when he saw his naked father. He ran to tell his brothers–expecting them to share in his entertainment. No wonder God said in His Word:

"For their feet run to evil, and make haste to shed blood."

Proverbs 1:16

Doesn't this sound familiar? What Ham did was no different from how some of us react today. As with Ham, some run to share gossip about another's sin or mistake. They get undue pleasure from someone else's downfall or vulnerable state. Satan uses this to expose or "uncover" the vulnerable person's sins and/or weaknesses. This could lead to the uncovered person's destruction as well as the destruction of the tale bearer.

Just listen to the news. It's sprinkled sparingly with good news and flooded with bad news. That's how Satan spreads his propaganda–through bad news. Uncovering another's sins is an abomination according to God. Read it for yourself.

"These six things doth the Lord hate: yea, seven are an abomination unto him:

A proud look, a lying tongue, and hands that shed innocent blood,

An heart that deviseth wicked imaginations, feet that be swift in running to mischief,

A false witness that speaketh lies, and he that soweth discord among brethren."

Proverbs 6:16-19

If these things are an abomination to God, they should be an abomination to us. If God covered our sins with His blood, we are to cover one another so that Satan does not get the advantage of us:

"Blessed is he whose transgression is forgiven, whose sin is covered."

Psalm 32:1

Ham's amusement and subsequent spiritual uncovering of his father resulted in a curse upon him. There are always consequences to our actions, so ensure that your actions correspond to the outcome that you desire.

Shem and Japheth chose to honor their father and covered him instead. Their actions resulted in blessings and honor. It all goes back to choosing life or death, blessing or cursing. I don't know about you, but I choose life which is synonymous with blessings! The love of God is made manifest in our lives when we choose to cover and protect one another:

"...but love covereth all sins."

Proverbs 10:12

God loves us so much that he covers us with His love. When he looks at us, He only sees His Son's blood. When you love someone, you value and protect them. As a matter of fact, when you value something you also protect it. There are many kinds of security in the world to protect people and things. Security systems include sensors that activate when the atmosphere is compromised.

So it is in the Spirit realm. When Satan attempts to invade our space, the Spirit of the Lord lifts up a standard against Him! The Holy Spirit activates the spiritual alarm, and the ministering spirits spring into action to cover and protect us! You can always tell the perceived worth of a person or thing by the amount of protection that surrounds them. Another clue is the length that thieves will go to in order to steal them! The reciprocal of that is if your perceived wealth is zero or very little, there would be little thought of trying to steal from you. You have nothing of value to offer.

God valued you so much that He gave His only begotten Son to die for you. Through Jesus' shed blood, we, the imperfect, became perfect!

"For by one offering, He hath perfected forever them that are sanctified."

Hebrews 10:14

To be sanctified is to be set apart for Him! Kings and queens don't dwell in ordinary houses and among ordinary people. They are set apart to live in palaces and among their own kind. You must be given a royal invitation to come in their presence. The amount of security that surrounds them attests to their status in life.

You have also been set apart as believers. We were given the royal invitation to "come to Jesus". When we accepted His invitation, we were given the privileges and benefits of royalty. We were set apart for Him, given security in Him and covered by His blood! You are His most valuable possession, and He ensures that His investments are well taken care of. His applied blood over you signifies to every demon spirit that you are off limits! Nothing shall by any means hurt you!

You are covered!

● ● ●

Confession

I am secure in my Father. I'm secure in His Word. Though I may sometimes walk in the valley of the shadow of death, I will fear no evil. God is with me. I am shielded by his shadow and nothing shall, by any means, harm me.

Psalm 91:10

There shall no evil befall thee, neither shall any plague come nigh thy dwelling.

● ● ●

Chapter 10
You Are Chosen

When the Board of Directors (BOD) of a well-known charitable organization in my area began to consider candidates for new board members, unknown to me, my name was submitted as a prospect. I served as a volunteer for several years and was content to remain in that modest role. Eventually, I was asked to join the BOD. I was extremely honored, while it was not a position that I sought.

Though I was confident that I could contribute to the company, I was a bit surprised at the offer. I was grateful that my volunteer work was recognized, but I truly had no desire to advance to a governing role. I only aspired to serve. Once I prayed about it and discussed it with my husband, I accepted the nomination.

I had been chosen.

You and I have been chosen by someone greater than any organization on earth. We were chosen by God Himself!

"For thou art an holy people unto the Lord thy God: the Lord thy God hath chosen thee to be a special people unto himself, above all people that are upon the

face of the earth."

Deuteronomy 7:6

When God looks at you, He only sees what He has chosen you to be. He has already spoken your destiny, and you are only living out the in-between (the process to destiny). The God of the entire universe chose mortal man to walk out His plan of salvation. It was also pretty incredulous to David, because he penned these words:

"What is man, that thou art mindful of him? And the son of man, that thou visitest him?"

Psalm 8:4

What do we have to offer Him that He chose us? The Lord unfolded this to me so that I could share with you the qualifications of son-ship. As you will see in this next scripture, we had no qualifications.

● ● ●

There is nothing you can offer God that will make Him love you more nor is there anything that you can do that will make Him love you less.

● ● ●

"But we are bound to give thanks alway to God for you, brethren beloved of the Lord, because God hath from the beginning chosen you to salvation through sanctification of the Spirit and belief of the truth."

2 Thessalonians 2:13

Pay close attention to "from the beginning". Before you or your forefathers were ever born, you were chosen—even before the foundation of the world. In case you think your special abilities, talents or charisma caused you to be chosen, think again. There is nothing you can offer God that will make Him love you more nor is there anything that you can do that will make Him love you less. You were chosen for His glory.

"This people have I formed for myself; they shall shew forth my praise."

Isaiah 43:21

He chose you on purpose.

"Moreover whom He did predestinate, them He also called: and whom He called, them He also justified: and whom He justified, them He also glorified."

Romans 8:30

You do not have to be qualified to be chosen. You were chosen to be qualified! God's way of doing things is far above our natural ways:

"For my thoughts are not your thoughts, neither are your ways my ways, saith the Lord.

For as the heavens are higher than the earth, so are my ways higher than your ways, and my thoughts than your thoughts."

Isaiah 55:8, 9

We often choose people based on their portfolios, looks, abilities, etc.

"...for man looketh on the outward appearance, but the Lord looketh on the heart."

1 Samuel 16:17

● ● ●

All God requires from us is for us to accept His offer to walk in our chosen-ness.

● ● ●

As earth dwellers, we do the best we can when it comes to making choices. We expect people to first be qualified. Then, they may or may not be chosen. All God requires from us is for us to accept His offer to walk in our chosen-ness. Your acceptance comes with all kinds of benefits! The way the world chooses you does not matter. The only qualification is that you simply say "yes" to His offer.

> *"But as many as received Him, to them gave He power to become the sons of God, even to them that believe on His name."*
>
> *John 1:12*

Have you accepted His offer? You are already chosen. All you have to do is say "yes!"

• • •
Confession

I am a chosen generation. I am a chosen vessel of God. God chose me even before I was born. I accept his offer and walk each day in my identity in Him.

John 15:16

Ye have not chosen me, but I have chosen you, and ordained you, that ye should go and bring forth fruit, and that your fruit should remain: whatsoever ye shall ask of the Father in my name, He may give it you.

• • •

Chapter 11
You Are An Overcomer

One of Satan's goals is to make you feel inferior. Because he can only work through the power of suggestion to our minds, will and emotions, he wants you to *feel* defeated every single day. Why does he try so hard? He knows that through Christ you are already victorious, but he works hard so that *you* won't identify with that truth. Satan glories in filling our lives with undue sorrow and rejection. However, there is good news! Jesus glories in making us an overcomer through Him!

• • •

Jesus has completely overwhelmed defeat.

• • •

To overcome means "to prevail over" or "to overpower." It means "to get the better of in a struggle or a conflict." John 16:33 states, *"These things I have spoken unto you, that in me ye might have peace. In the world ye shall have tribulation: but be of good cheer; I have overcome the world."* Don't miss the revelation of this scripture. You *will* experience tough times on earth. But, with God, you can be happy because in Him is peace! Jesus has completely overwhelmed defeat. With God we can conquer *anything*, for

Jesus has already purchased our success! If you are a believer, you are an overcomer!

In Chapter 7, we discussed what an heir meant and all the entitlements as a result of lineage. We also established that you are a joint heir with Jesus Christ and that you automatically receive all the benefits of that lineage. It is important that you understand that not only has Christ overcome the world through his death, burial and resurrection, but we also have inherited the title of "Overcomer" through our lineage in Him *"...as He is, so are we in this world."* (1 John 4:17)

Our adversary (Satan) knows that he has already lost the battle and that death no longer has a sting to those who are believers. So, he endeavors to keep you in a defeated mentality. He knows the Scriptures as well or better than we do, so he knows that Prov. 23:7 states, *"For as he thinketh in his heart, so is he."* He uses the Scriptures for his purposes, and if he can get you to think opposite to what the Word says you are, he has accomplished his purpose.

● ● ●

When you think with a defeatist mentality, you will *live* in defeat.

● ● ●

When you think with a defeatist mentality, you will *live* in defeat. Satan does not want you to LIVE in victory! He wants you to LIVE in defeat! Satan wants to keep you from moving forward. God wants you to live, move and have your being in Him! Satan wants you to feel rejection, depression and oppression. God wants you to have life and that more abundantly!

Should we roll over and play dead when Satan comes against us? The Apostle Paul said a resounding "no!" Romans 8:37 says, *"Nay, in all these things we are more than conquerors through him that loved us."* I had to understand why the Word was written that way. Why does it say we are "more" than conquerors. To have more of something means to abound in that thing. You have more than enough–more than what you need.

You have a multitude of something. You have plenty! The Greek definition for "more" in this scripture is "to gain a decisive victory." In other words, there will be no question as to who won the battle because the person who wins will have the spoils!

I hope you see where I'm going.

You don't just have enough victory to get through one problem or situation. You have more than enough to handle anything that you face. Jesus put "more" into you. As I meditate on this revelation, I am reminded of Numbers 13:30, *"Let us go up at once, and possess it; for we are well able to overcome it."* Here, Moses was speaking to his people about what seemed like an insurmountable circumstance. In spite of the dilemma, Moses understood the power that they had on their side. Not only do you have more, but you are "well able" to overcome any obstacle that you may face in this life.

You may wonder "in what things am I more than a conqueror?" Let's review a couple of passages from Romans 8. Verses 35-36 reads: *"Who shall separate us from the love of Christ? Shall tribulation, or distress, or persecution, or famine, or nakedness, or peril, or sword? As it is written, For thy sake we are killed all the day long; we are accounted as sheep for the slaughter."*

I love the way Matthew Henry interprets this passage: *"Whatever believers may be separated from, enough remains. None can take Christ from the believer: none can take the believer from Him; and that is enough. All other hazards signify nothing."*[1]

As I stated at the beginning, Satan has plots and suggestions designed to keep you in bondage and the agony of defeat. The Bible says that we are *"accounted as sheep for the slaughter."* Every day there is a new tactic designed to attack the

---

[1] Matthew Henry Concise Commentary. Retrieved December 08, 2009 from christnotes.org. Website: http://www.christnotes.org/commentary.

truth. *"But thanks be unto God, which always causeth us to triumph in Christ, and maketh manifest the savour of His knowledge by us in every place."* (2 Corinthians 2:14)

Tribulation, distress, persecution, famine (limited resources), nakedness, peril or sword...these things constantly come against you to pull you from your pedestal of victory. However, these "hazards signify nothing" as they can do nothing to separate you from God's love in Christ Jesus. Be of good cheer! Christ has overcome the world! As He is, so are you!

• • •

Confession

Defeat is not an option in my life as I live in victory. The one who overcame the world lives within me. I am empowered by the Word of God which says that in all things I am more than a conqueror. This is the victory that I have as a believer.

1 John 5:4

For whatsoever is born of God overcometh the world; and this is the victory that overcometh the world, even our faith.

• • •

Chapter 12
You Are Worthy

Recently, I was listening to one of my favorite Christian artists, CeCe Winans. One song in particular caught my attention, as it confirmed the message of this book. As I listened to the lyrics of "Worthy" from the album *Thy Kingdom Come,* I was reminded of another truth about our identities in Christ. The lyrics go on to say that "You're counted as worthy, so let's be worthy." You were counted as worthy when God sent His Son to die for you, now BE worthy!

Often, because of life's situations, disappointments, and mistakes of the past, we don't think we are worthy of anything good. We don't think we are worthy of happiness. We don't think we're worthy of God's grace and favor. Consequently, when we don't have any sense of *worth*, we don't expect anything *good*. We continue to live in expectation of mediocrity in every area because our expectation is only in what we think we deserve. When unfavorable things happen in our lives, we assume that we are reaping our worth or what we deserve.

> • • •
> **When we don't have any sense of *worth*, we don't expect anything *good*.**
> • • •

For example, when you interview for a job, the salary that you are offered may be based on your credentials and years of experience. When I interviewed for my first job after college, the salary that I was offered was pretty low. I actually expected that. My credentials weren't very impressive, because I had very little on-the-job experience and a very new college degree to offer.

That's how many of us erroneously feel about God's grace. We feel that our credentials have to be stacked to benefit from God's love. We feel that we have to be the best at everything–the best wife or husband, mother or father, employee, church member, etc. This is contrary to what the Bible teaches. Grace is God's favor that cannot be earned. If you have to earn it, Christ died in vain.

● ● ●

Grace is God's favor that cannot be earned.

● ● ●

God did not choose us because of our "impressive" credentials. There is nothing that we can offer to qualify us for salvation. Simply put, we are not qualified–we are justified. We have been absolved of all guilt. No longer are we to blame. As a result of what Christ did for us, we are now worthy.

The very act of God sending His only begotten Son to die for our sins shows us that we are worthy. We are so valuable to Him that He sacrificed His only Son's life to bring us back into right standing with Him. We all know the story of the crucifixion. If you saw *The Passion of the Christ*, you witnessed the grim and horrifying depiction of Christ's slow, degrading and painful death. Would you die for someone who was not worthy of your death? Scripture says that *while we were yet sinners, Christ died for us.* Jesus endured a shameful death, despising the shame, just so we could be made worthy.

Even though you are worthy, you may not feel worthy. You may ask, how can I be worthy of God's love and have good things happen in my life when I see nothing but adverse circumstances all around me? In order to "be" anything, you must take on its characteristics. You have to exist within the context of that thing. To exist in worthiness (know that you are truly worthy), you must allow the water of the Word to change the way you think.

> *"Finally, brethren, whatsoever things are honest, whatsoever things are just, whatsoever things are pure, whatsoever things are lovely, whatsoever things are of good report; if there be any virtue, and if there be any praise, think on these things."*
>
> *Philippians 4:8*

Don't take on the *victim* mentality. It will only keep you from living the life of victory for which you are counted worthy. *Do* take on the *victor* mentality. Meditate on things that give you peace and joy and that create a thankful heart. Delight in God's Word, confess it over and over, and you will find that everything God says you are, you will become within and without.

As I contemplate our worthiness, is there anybody who is truly worthy (the way we think of worthiness) of receiving anything from the Lord? Think about it. We were born and shaped in iniquity. We may not walk in obedience every day. We sometimes have prideful spirits. We sometimes walk in unbelief of God's Word. We've done so many things that we think disappoint the Lord; so, we may feel *discounted* as worthy. I have good news for you. When the Father looks at us, He only sees the blood of His Son, Jesus! We could never obey our way into Heaven. We could never pray our way into Heaven. We are only worthy of Heaven through the blood of Jesus. That's dancing news!

You were counted as worthy before you even arrived on the scene. The Lord has always been mindful of us. (Psalm 115:12). He offered up His Son–the most perfect lamb without blemish–as a sacrifice to bridge the enormous gap between us and Him. The ocean of sin would have kept us from ever being redeemed to our Father if Jesus had not died. We are now worthy of every benefit as a joint heir with Christ through His blood.

Denounce every lie that tells you anything contrary to what Jesus said. *"Cast down imaginations and every high thing that exalteth itself against the knowledge of God, and bring into captivity every thought to the obedience of Christ."* (2 Corinthians 10:5). That's right. You have to do some work–not to stay worthy–but to shake in the devil's face that you are worthy when he comes with his lies. God has given us power through His Word to be victorious in every area of struggle.

Once you receive this truth in your very spirit, no devil in nor out of hell can keep you from walking in your authority. "Truth" is a person. Jesus said, *"I am the way, the truth, and the life."* (John 14:6). When you receive truth, you receive Jesus, God and the Word! Once you *know* the truth, Scripture says truth makes you free. (John 8:32). Continue to meditate that Jesus (the truth and the Word) said that you are worthy, because he made you worthy. Cast down the lies of Satan and receive and elevate God's Word which brings light. Allow the Word of God to illuminate your path (life). *"Thy Word is a lamp unto my feet, and a light unto my path."* (Psalm 119:105)

● ● ●

God's truths and plans for you are eternal.

● ● ●

Because we live in this world, we may all feel unworthy at various times in our lives. The circumstances we face, and the unwise decisions we may have made sometimes paint a bleak picture. Your current conditions may give you a false impression of who you are. During these times, remember that you are worthy through the blood of Jesus. Check out 2 Corinthians 4:18: *"For we look **not** at the things **which are seen**, but at the things **which are not seen**: for the things **which are seen** are **temporal**; but the things **which are not seen** are **eternal**."* To put it in laymen's terms, there is more to see than what meets the eye. Everything you're dealing with now is subject to change! It's only temporary. God's truths and plans for you are eternal. Not just in Heaven. Here. Now!

Remember. Anything contrary to the Word of God is a lie. Don't believe it. Believe and receive the truth of God's Word. The truth is that you're counted worthy...so BE worthy. Be victorious. Be healthy. Be prosperous. Be who you were destined to be. In the words of CeCe Winans, "it doesn't matter how you feel, but what is right–that is real!"

You're valuable, you matter, and you are worthy!

• • •

Confession

I have been counted as worthy! I am worthy of God's grace and love. I am worthy of His good pleasure and goodness. I will not allow feelings of inadequacy to dominate my mind, but I will cast down every lie that is contrary to the Word of God, which is His ultimate truth.

Psalm 8:4

What is man, that thou art mindful of him? And the son of man, that thou visitest him?

• • •

True You Confessions

৪০৪০৪০

Today, I discard forever the negative images that have shaped my identity for too long. From this day forward I walk and live in my true identity–understanding that God's purpose for my life is for me to walk in peace and victory. His purpose is for me to prosper physically, mentally, emotionally, spiritually and financially.

৪০৪০৪০

I am the Righteousness of God!

I am the righteousness of God in Him (Jesus). I am clothed in His righteousness. I no longer wear the ugly and weighty garments of sin and of my past. I am a new creation in Christ Jesus. I have been set free from bondage, and I now live a new and victorious life.

৪০৪০৪০

I am Beautiful!

I am fearfully and wonderfully made. I am a work of art–crafted and drafted by the master craftsman. I was made in the image of the AWESOME Creator, and everything that God made is *good!* The Lord is pleased with me. He looks upon me with love and affection. I can **boldly** live my life knowing that God's loving gaze is always upon me.

৪০৪০৪০

I am a Friend!

I am a friend of God. He loves me and values his connection with me. He is my confidante. He reveals His heart to me. Our special friendship confirms my identity and gives me hope for the future. I look forward to each day that we share together in this life and the life to come.

ಬಿಬಿಬಿ

I am Anointed!

I am anointed. I carry the Anointing within me. Because He dwells within me, the oil of God's anointing flows through every area of my life. It is an honor and a pleasure to have His presence in me. I will treasure this wonderful gift for the rest of my life. I will keep my temple Holy and will purposefully protect this sacred gift.

ಬಿಬಿಬಿ

I am Free!

I am free! I am no longer bound by darkness. I no longer have shackles on me. I have been set free from the bondage of sin and its effects that hinder my growth. From this day forward, I live a joyous and purposeful life. I am no longer bound by depression, shame, hurt, disappointment, misery and defeat. I now live a life of blessings, contentment, joy, peace and freedom. Today, I choose life!

ಬಿಬಿಬಿ

I am Blessed!

I am blessed! God's Word says that I'm blessed in the city and the fields. Everywhere I go, I'm blessed. When the sun rises and sets, I'm blessed. Despite what may be happening in my life, I'm blessed. I will rest in the truth of God's Word. I will not waiver in unbelief. I will hold fast to His promises.

৪৩৪৩৪৩

I am Royalty!

I am royalty. I have been supernaturally adopted into a royal family by my faith in Jesus Christ. I will no longer accept a poverty mentality. I will embrace my royal status as a joint heir with Jesus Christ. I will live in earnest expectation of the blessings that I am destined to receive as a born-again believer.

৪৩৪৩৪৩

I am Favored!

My Father has plans for me. His favor is all around me. I walk in His favor. I can do all things through Christ as He strengthens and favors me!

৪৩৪৩৪৩

I am Covered!

I am secure in my Father. I'm secure in His Word. Though I may sometimes walk in the valley of the shadow of death,

I will fear no evil. God is with me. I am shielded by his shadow and nothing shall, by any means, harm me.

૨૦૪૦૪૦

I am Chosen!

I am a chosen generation. I am a chosen vessel of God. God chose me even before I was born. I accept his offer and walk each day in my identity in Him.

૨૦૪૦૪૦

I am An Overcomer!

Defeat is not an option in my life as I live in victory. The one who overcame the world lives within me. I am empowered by the Word of God which says that in all things I am more than a conqueror. This is the victory that I have as a believer.

૨૦૪૦૪૦

I am Worthy!

I have been counted as worthy! I am worthy of God's grace and love. I am worthy of His good pleasure and goodness. I will not allow feelings of inadequacy to dominate my mind, but I will cast down every lie that is contrary to the Word of God, which is His ultimate truth.

૨૦૪૦૪૦

Also available by Author, *Yakisha T. Simmons*:

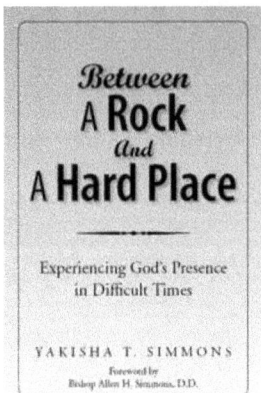

ISBN: 978-1-4257-8235-1

Available for purchase at:
www.barnesandnoble.com

For a signed copy and additional information:
www.yakishasimmons.com

www.lifechangersenterprise.com

For speaking or book signing engagements, contact:

Jonathan Simmons
843-425-9568